Hosting with
The Lazy Makoti

A celebration of food

MOGAU SESHOENE

Jonathan Ball Publishers
Johannesburg • Cape Town • London

This book is dedicated to Mama Dorah Sitole, an ode to your love and incredible legacy. It has been my greatest pleasure to know and learn from you. I cherish every moment spent. I will love and miss you always. Robala ka khutšo.

Contents

V vegetarian

Forewords

Mogau and I first met over tea in Maboneng years ago, when she shared with me her story of food and how The Lazy Makoti began. Her vision was to travel through your kitchens, sharing recipes and the aromas and flavours of her childhood, to preserve her food heritage.

Over the last year I've been privileged and humbled to have spent a few months mentoring her in food-styling techniques, brand immersion and media to assist her in building her own brand. During that time, she and I formed a very special and unique relationship, for which I'm so grateful. I'm so thrilled to have her in my life.

Everything Mogau does, she does with passion, from her live Instagram cookalongs to her recipes. She oozes warmth and energy, and it's infectious. I can't wait to see how her unique characteristics and irrepressible enthusiasm flood the pages of this book, visiting the traditional and glimpsing the new.

'Bless the food before us, the family beside us, and the love between us.'

Abigail Donnelly
Woolworths head food creative and *Woolworths Taste* food director

Mogau, I celebrate you and I'm very proud of what you've put together. This is not just a cookbook, but a demonstration of what one can achieve with passion.

I remember like yesterday the day in 2014 when we had that first meeting in my office – I knew this was the beginning of an industry disruptor and greatness. What a journey it has been to watch you grow and master your craft. Your passion and discipline are the cornerstones of the legacy you're building, and I'm happy to be part of it.

Love you always!

Savita K Mbuli
Businesswoman

When a meal takes you back to the very first big family gathering you ever feasted at or to your grandmother's daily menu and treats, it becomes more than just nourishment. That meal is joy on a plate. Mogau's way with food puts beautiful labels on age-old foods that have been passed from generation to generation, foods that have generally not been given space on fine-dining menus. She's very intentional in how she centres her work around indigenous foods, giving them the high status they deserve.

Mogau reminds us of the versatility of the produce we grew up with. She also shows us that we can play around with the classics and give them new shapes and flavours. As someone who holds our heritage in high regard, it brings me comfort to know that there are young people who are dedicated to elevating the indigenous foods of this country to their rightful place on the main table of the South African food scene.

Watching Mogau and her brand blossom has left me with nothing but pride. I look at her work and listen to her speak, and know that when the late doyenne of African cooking, Dorah Sitole, gave us *Cooking from Cape to Cairo* many years ago, she planted a seed that fell on fertile ground. I can't wait to try out the new recipes and feed my loved ones the joy in these pages.

O dira mošomo o bohlokwa kudu, Mogau. Re a go leboga.

Florence Masebe
Actor, writer and producer

The commitment to celebrating South Africa's rich and diverse cultural heritage is firmly fixed in our people's spirit. The establishment of The Lazy Makoti by chef Mogau Seshoene in 2014 was a wonderful contribution to the celebration of South African heritage through cuisine.

Our food tells stories of what defines us: creatively expressed in distinctive flavours, it remains true to our origins. Passed down from generation to generation, it celebrates what sets South Africa apart from the rest of the world.

The Lazy Makoti shares her patriotism and pride in this heritage through our favourite traditional cuisines. Through the medium of food, Chef Seshoene is truly inspiring new ways of preserving our heritage.

Brand South Africa

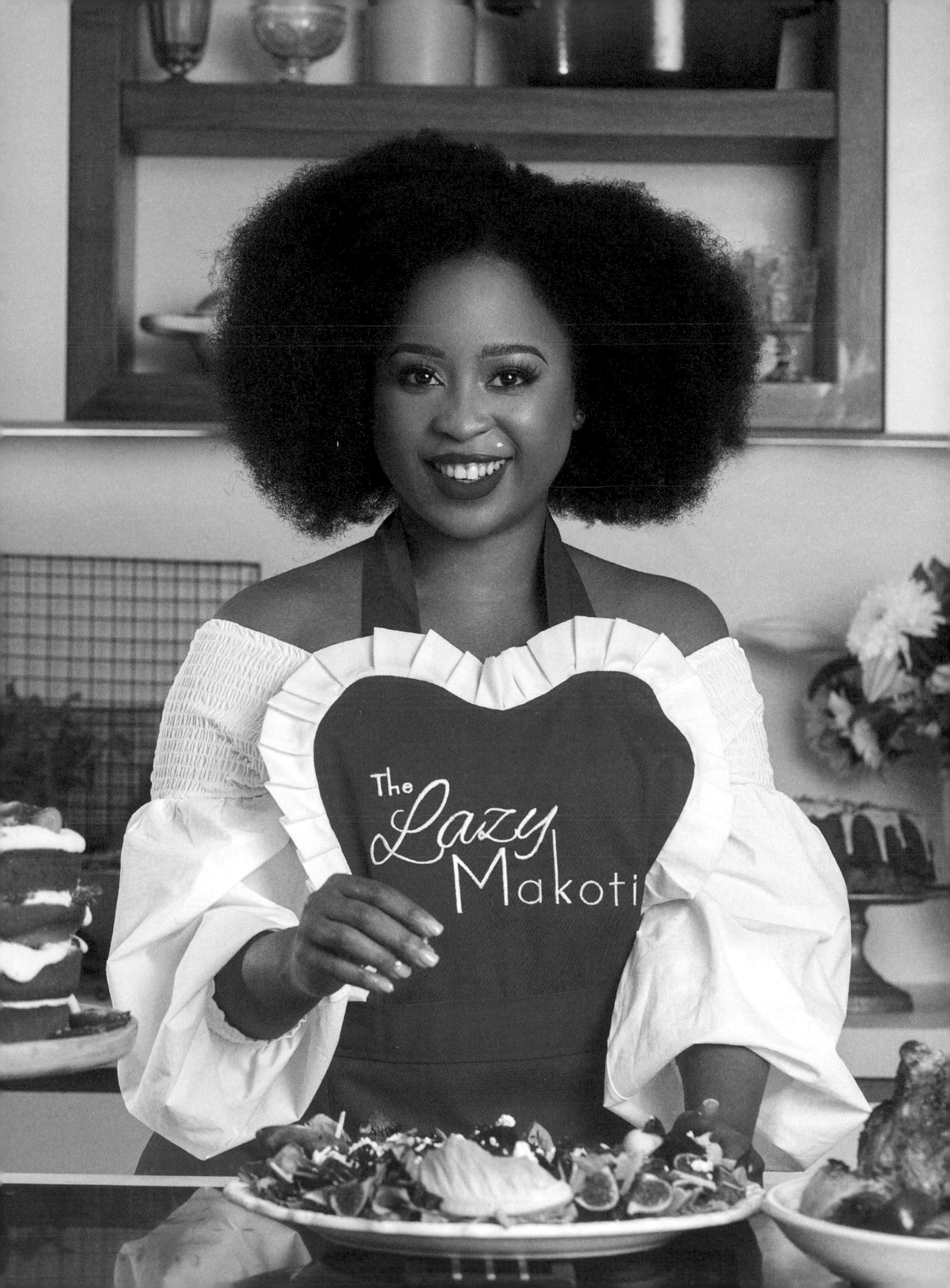
The Lazy Makoti

Introduction

This book is a culmination of many moments shared with my community – and by that I mean you, reading this right now. From interactions on social media, in comments sections, inboxes and DMs, through emails and conversations in cooking classes, and exchanges during IG live cookalongs, through the time spent together on the internet to help get each other through lockdown, we cooked and baked, laughed, and shared meals and recipes. And through all that I was busy, noting every recipe that caught your attention, every recipe you constantly requested and asked about, every recipe I made and loved. I have never enjoyed any process more.

These recipes were carefully and thoughtfully considered, for you. There are simple breakfasts and weekday dinners that save on time but deliver on deliciousness, special weekend recipes for entertaining, hearty winter meals and the perfect Sunday-lunch spread. And I've included a plant-based chapter that will surprise and impress everyone! There are easy bakes and desserts to finish any meal and, of course, chapters that celebrate traditional South African and African food, our heritage that is my greatest love. The final chapter is an amazing array of recipes that will definitely find their place on your celebration table: from birthdays to Valentine's Day, Easter to Christmas, you are absolutely sorted!

Get ready to impress with tried-and-tested recipes that are easy to follow and leave everyone begging for seconds. Prepare to be everyone's favourite! #ThankMeLater

Because most people use cups and spoons to measure, and not a scale, most converted measurements (in brackets) are provided in ml.

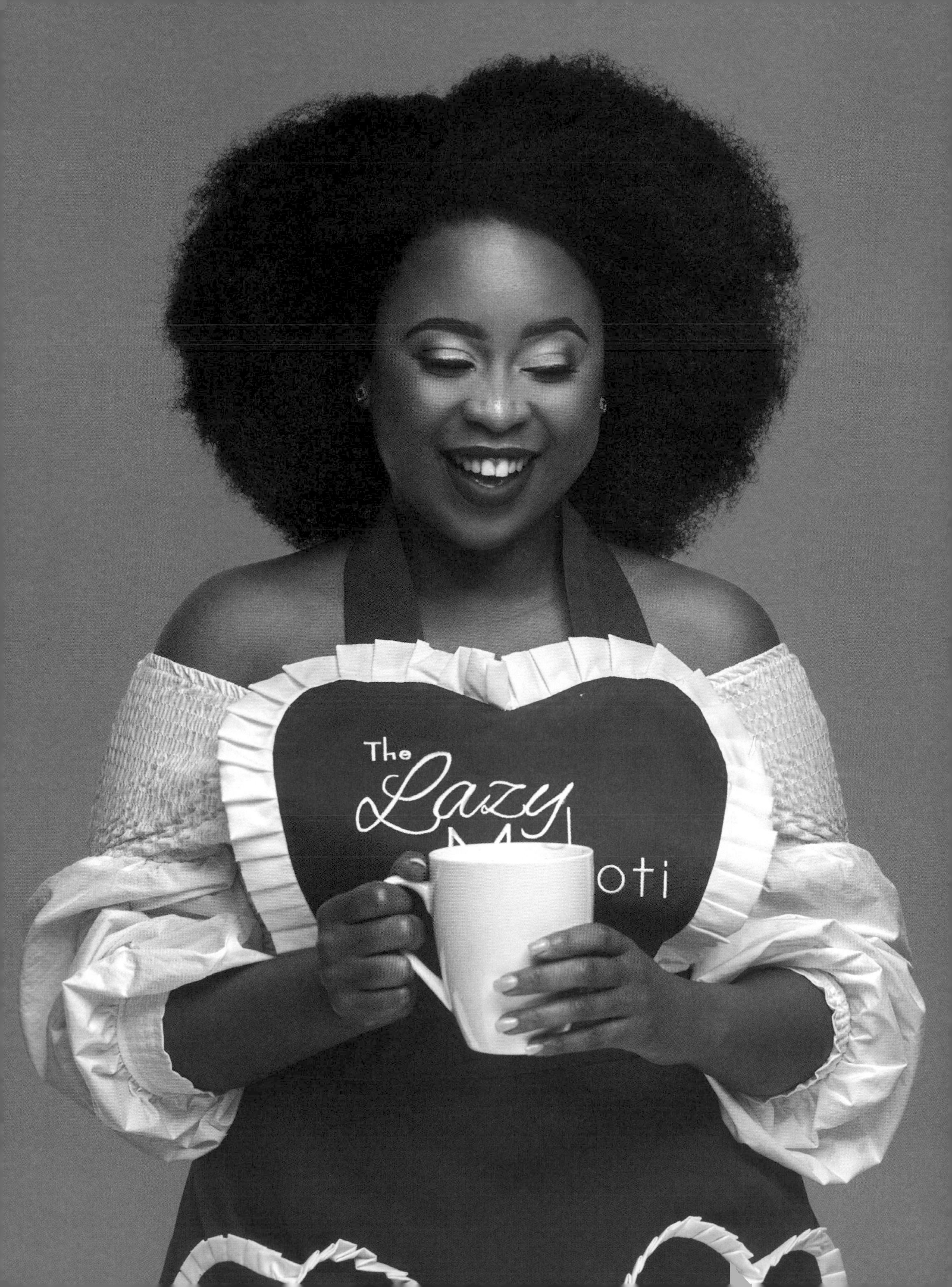
The
Lazy
oti

1

Top of the morning

Everything breakfast. Simple and delicious recipes to start the day.

Amasi and bran rusks

Prep time: 15 minutes
Baking time: 1 hour plus 6 hours drying
Makes: 30 rusks

Ingredients

4 cups wholewheat flour

2½ cups (625 ml) All Bran Flakes

2½ cups (625 ml) instant oats

2 tablespoons (30 ml) baking powder

1 cup (250 ml) castor sugar

½ teaspoon (2½ ml) salt

½ cup (125 ml) seed mix (sunflower seeds, pumpkin seeds, chia seeds)

2 cups (500 ml) amasi

2 eggs

¾ cup (190 ml) water

½ cup (125 ml) vegetable oil

1 teaspoon (5 ml) vanilla essence

1. Preheat oven to 180 °C. Grease two loaf tins.
2. In a large bowl combine the flour, All Bran Flakes, oats, baking powder, sugar, salt and seed mix. Combine well.
3. In a separate bowl, whisk together amasi, eggs, water, oil and vanilla essence.
4. Pour wet mixture into dry mixture, and mix until well combined.
5. Spoon into loaf tins. Bake until skewer inserted comes out clean, 50-60 minutes.
6. Remove from oven and leave to cool in the tins for 20 minutes, then turn out onto a chopping board.
7. Cut into 30 rusks and place on a baking tray. Dry out in 100 °C oven for 6 hours with the oven door slightly ajar.

Lemon and poppy-seed muffins

These are among my favourite muffins to make and to enjoy with a cup of hot tea. I just love the flavour and that they aren't too sweet – my mother loves them too, and she always prefers a medium sweetness. Poppy seeds can be found in most grocery stores and health shops.

Prep time: 20 minutes
Baking time: 20 minutes
Makes: 12 muffins

Ingredients

2 cups (500 ml) cake flour
2 teaspoons (10 ml) baking powder
3 tablespoons (45 ml) poppy seeds
½ cup (125 ml) butter, at room temperature
½ cup (125 ml) castor sugar
2 eggs
zest and juice of 2 lemons
½ cup (125 ml) buttermilk or plain yoghurt
½ teaspoon (2½ ml) bicarbonate of soda

For the glaze:
juice of 2 lemons or ½ cup (125 ml) lemon juice
2 tablespoons (30 ml) icing sugar

1. Preheat oven to 180 ˚C. Line muffin tray with paper muffin cases.
2. Put the flour, baking powder and poppy seeds in a large bowl. Combine well.
3. In a separate bowl, cream butter and castor sugar till fluffy and pale, about 10 minutes with an electric beater.
4. Add eggs, lemon zest and juice, buttermilk and bicarbonate of soda, and mix well.
5. Tip wet ingredients into dry ingredients and combine well.
6. Fill muffin cases three-quarters full.
7. Bake for 20 minutes.
8. Remove from oven and transfer to wire cooling rack.
9. Combine glaze ingredients and drizzle a little over each muffin.

Three-ingredient peanut-butter biscuits

Prep time: 10 minutes
Baking time: 10-12 minutes
Makes: 10-12 biscuits

(V) Ingredients

1 cup (250 ml) peanut butter
1 egg, beaten
½ cup (125 ml) castor sugar

1. Preheat oven to 180 °C. Grease a baking tray.
2. Put the peanut butter, egg and castor sugar in a bowl and mix until well combined.
3. Roll into small balls of equal size. Lay out on baking tray with enough space between each for a bit of spreading. Press the top of each ball with the back of a fork to flatten it slightly.
4. Bake for 10-12 minutes.
5. Remove from oven and leave to cool for a few minutes before transferring to cooling rack. Leave to cool completely.

Tip: Add ½ cup (125 ml) oats to make the biscuits extra crunchy and nutritious.

Breakfast egg burger

Prep time: 20 minutes
Cooking time: 10-20 minutes
Serves: 4

Ingredients

1 tablespoon (15 ml) butter
4-6 eggs, beaten
8 rashers bacon
4 burger buns
mayonnaise for spreading
handful rocket
1 red onion, sliced
1 cup (250 ml) grated cheese

1. Heat the butter in a frying pan, and cook the eggs to desired doneness. Set aside.
2. Fry the bacon till crispy and cooked. Set aside.
3. Cut open each burger bun and spread it with mayo.
4. On each bun, layer rocket, bacon, slices of red onion and eggs.
5. Sprinkle cheese over. Top with the other half of the bun.

Spicy mince shakshuka

Prep time: 10 minutes
Cooking time: 35 minutes
Serves: 4

Ingredients

2 tablespoons (30 ml) olive oil
1 onion, diced
1 teaspoon (5 ml) crushed garlic
½ red pepper, diced
½ yellow pepper, diced
½ green pepper, diced
2 teaspoons (10 ml) curry powder
500 g mincemeat
1 teaspoon (5 ml) steak and chops spice
1-2 red chillies, finely chopped (optional)
2 tomatoes, grated
1 teaspoon (5 ml) sugar
4 eggs
coriander to garnish

1. In a large cast-iron pan, heat the olive oil. Sauté the onion, garlic and peppers for 2-3 minutes.
2. Add the curry powder and sauté till fragrant, 2-3 minutes.
3. Add the mincemeat and spice, and chopped chillies if using, and sauté till mince is browned, about 10 minutes.
4. Preheat oven to 180 ˚C.
5. Add the grated tomato and sugar to the mince, and simmer until the mixture thickens, 10-15 minutes.
6. Using the back of a spoon, make 4 indentations in the mince and crack an egg into each.
7. Transfer to the oven and bake until the egg is cooked and set, about 5 minutes.
8. Garnish with chopped coriander.

Breakfast smoothies

**Prep time: 10 minutes
Serves: 2-4**

Ⓥ Mixed-berry smoothie

1 cup (250 ml) blueberries
1 cup (250 ml) strawberries
½ cup (125 ml) raspberries
1 banana, cut into chunks
1 cup (250 ml) plain yoghurt
1 cup (250 ml) milk

1. Place the ingredients in a blender and blend to a smooth consistency.

Ⓥ Green smoothie

1 frozen banana
½ cup (125 ml) raw chopped spinach
½ cup (125 ml) milk
1 cup (250 ml) plain yoghurt

1. Place the ingredients in a blender and blend to a smooth consistency.

Ⓥ Peanut-butter smoothie

2 frozen bananas
½ cup (125 ml) milk
1 cup (250 ml) plain yoghurt
6 tablespoons (90 ml) peanut butter

1. Place the ingredients in a blender and blend to a smooth consistency.

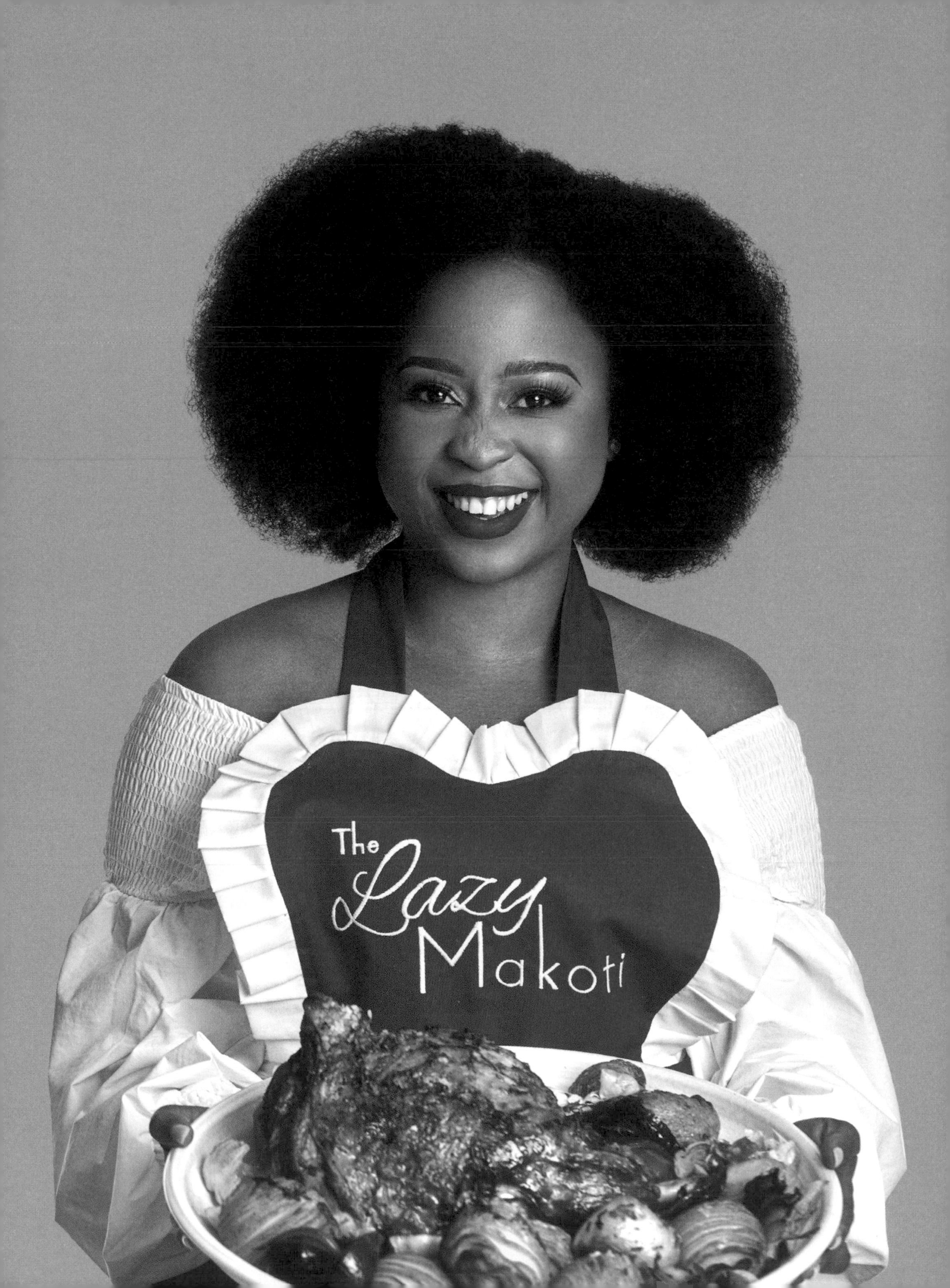
The Lazy Makoti

2

Dinner's ready

Convenient and quick meals, ready in minutes at the end of a busy day: the perfect plates to put on a family dinner table.

One-pot chicken and rice

*The easiest, most delicious chicken-and-rice dish you've ever tasted!
Don't worry if you don't have a cast-iron pot – just transfer the rice
to an oven-safe dish for baking.*

**Prep time: 15 minutes
Cooking time: 1 hour
Serves: 4-6**

Ingredients

4-6 chicken thighs
3 tablespoons (45 ml) olive oil
1 finely chopped onion
**1 teaspoon (5 ml) minced
   garlic**
2 carrots, finely cubed
½ red pepper, diced
½ yellow pepper, diced
½ green pepper, diced
1½ cups (375 ml) rice
**2¼ cups (560 ml) chicken
   stock**
salt and pepper to taste
parsley to garnish

For the spice rub:

**1 teaspoon (5 ml) garlic
   powder**
½ teaspoon (2½ ml) paprika
**1 teaspoon (5 ml) barbecue
   spice**
**1 teaspoon (5 ml) lemon and
   herb spice**

1. Preheat oven to 180 °C.
2. Combine the spice-rub ingredients in a large bowl. Add the chicken thighs and toss to coat evenly.
3. In a large cast-iron pan, heat 2 tablespoons (30 ml) of the olive oil and fry the chicken thighs to brown, 2-3 minutes on each side. Remove and set aside.
4. Add 1 tablespoon (15 ml) oil to same pan, and sauté the onion and garlic for 1 minute. Add the carrots and peppers, and fry to soften.
5. Add the rice and chicken stock, stir, and simmer for 5 minutes.
6. Put the thighs back into the pot with their juices, and season with salt and pepper. Bring to a simmer and cover.
7. Place in the oven for 30 minutes (or cook on the stove top). Remove the lid and bake until the liquid is absorbed, about 10 minutes.
8. Garnish with parsley.

Lentil and potato curry

Prep time: 15 minutes
Cooking time: 40 minutes
Serves: 4

Ingredients

2 tablespoons (30 ml) olive oil

1 onion, chopped

1 teaspoon (5 ml) minced garlic

1 teaspoon (5 ml) minced ginger

1 teaspoon (5 ml) turmeric

1 teaspoon (5 ml) cumin

2 tomatoes, grated

1 cup (250 ml) lentils, washed

2 potatoes, peeled and cubed

1½-2 cups (375-500 ml) water

½ tin coconut milk

coriander to garnish

1. Heat the oil in a large pot and sauté the onion for 1 minute. Add the garlic, ginger and spices, and fry till fragrant, 2-3 minutes.
2. Add the tomato and simmer, stirring a few times, for 5 minutes.
3. Add the lentils and potatoes, plus 1 cup (250 ml) water, and bring to the boil. Reduce heat to low, cover pot and leave to simmer until lentils are tender and mixture has thickened, about 25 minutes. Stir occasionally to prevent the lentils from sticking to the bottom. If the curry starts to look dry, add extra ½-1 cup (125-250 ml) water.
4. Stir in the coconut milk.
5. Garnish with coriander and serve with Easy flatbread (recipe on next page).

Easy flatbread

Prep time: 15 minutes
Cooking time: 25 minutes
Makes: 4

Ⓥ Ingredients

- **1¾ cups (440 ml) self-raising flour, plus extra for rolling**
- **1 cup (250 ml) plain yoghurt**
- **½ teaspoon (2½ ml) salt**
- **2 teaspoons (10 ml) melted butter (optional)**

1. In a large mixing bowl, combine the flour, yoghurt and salt. Mix well to combine.
2. Lightly flour a surface and turn the dough out onto it. Knead it for 8 minutes. Divide into four even portions. Flatten each portion to a thickness of about 2 cm using a roller.
3. Heat a pan on medium heat and dry-fry each round for 2-3 minutes on each side.
4. Brush each side of the cooked flatbread lightly with melted butter if desired. (Illustrated on previous page.)

Note: You can double all ingredient quantities to make 8 flatbreads.

Herby dombolo

Prep time: 10 minutes plus 30 minutes for rising
Cooking time: 1 hour
Makes: 6

Ⓥ Ingredients

4 cups (1 litre) flour
1 packet instant dry yeast
1½ teaspoons (7½ ml) sugar
1 teaspoon (5 ml) salt
¼ cup (60 ml) finely
   chopped fresh herbs
   (parsley, rosemary, basil)
2½ cups (625 ml) water
oil for greasing

1. Put all the dry ingredients into a large bowl and combine well.
2. Make a well in the centre and add the water. Combine well and knead until elastic, about 8 minutes. Form into a large ball.
3. Grease a bowl with a little oil. Place the dough in the bowl and cover with a cloth. Place in a warm spot and allow to rise until double in size, about 30 minutes.
4. Knock down dough by gently punching it to deflate it, and divide into 6 ramekins.
5. Add a little water to a large pot. Place ramekins on bottom of pot.
6. Bring to a simmer and steam till cooked through or until skewer inserted comes out clean, about 1 hour. (Illustrated on next page.)

Chicken curry

Prep time: 15 minutes
Cooking time: 30 minutes
Serves: 4-6

Ingredients

1 tablespoon (15 ml) oil
1 tablespoon (15 ml) butter
1 onion, chopped
1 teaspoon (5 ml) minced
   garlic
1 teaspoon (5 ml) minced
   ginger
2 tablespoons (30 ml)
   curry powder
4 chicken breasts, cubed
2 tablespoons (30 ml)
   tomato paste
¼ cup (60 ml) water
salt and pepper to taste
¼ cup (60 ml) fresh cream
finely chopped coriander to
   garnish (optional)

1. In a large saucepan, heat the oil and butter on medium heat. Add the onion and sauté for 2-3 minutes.
2. Add the garlic, ginger and curry powder. Fry till fragrant, 2-3 minutes, ensuring it doesn't burn.
3. Add the chicken and toss to coat.
4. Add the tomato paste and water, and cook till the chicken is just done, 10-15 minutes. Season with salt and pepper.
5. Stir in the cream and simmer for 10 minutes.
6. Garnish with chopped coriander and serve with Herby dombolo (recipe on previous page).

Pineapple and ginger lamb chops

Prep time: 10 minutes
Cooking time: 30 minutes
Serves: 4-6

Ingredients

1 tablespoon (15 ml) paprika
1 tablespoon (15 ml) steak
and chops spice
1 teaspoon (5 ml) black
pepper
6-8 lamb chops
oil for frying

For the glaze:

½ cup (125 ml) syrup from
tinned pineapple
1 teaspoon (5 ml) minced
garlic
1 teaspoon (5 ml) minced
ginger
2 tablespoons (30 ml) soy
sauce
1 tablespoon (15 ml) honey

1. In a small bowl, combine the paprika, steak and chops spice and black pepper. Rub generously over lamb chops.
2. In a pan, heat the oil and fry the chops till brown, 3-5 minutes on each side. Remove from pan and set aside.
3. Add all the glaze ingredients to the same pan and bring to a gentle simmer on low heat. Simmer until thickened, 5-10 minutes.
4. Return the chops to the pan and cook for 4-5 minutes on each side.

Smothered pork chops

Prep time: 10 minutes
Cooking time: 25 minutes
Serves: 4

Ingredients

2 tablespoons (30 ml)
   olive oil
4 pork chops
salt and pepper to taste
1 tablespoon (15 ml) butter
1 onion, chopped
1 teaspoon (5 ml) minced
   garlic
1 cup (250 ml) sliced
   mushrooms
few sprigs fresh thyme
½ cup (125 ml) chicken stock
½ cup (125 ml) fresh cream

1. Heat the oil in a large pan over medium heat. Season the pork chops generously with salt and pepper. Fry for 3-5 minutes on each side. Remove from pan and set aside.
2. Melt the butter in the same pan. Add the onion and garlic and fry till soft, 2-3 minutes.
3. Add the mushrooms and thyme and fry to soften, about 5 minutes.
4. Add the chicken stock and simmer for 2-3 minutes.
5. Reduce heat and add the cream.
6. Put the pork chops back into the pan and cook until heated through, about 5 minutes.
7. Serve with The perfect mash (recipe on next page).

The perfect mash

Prep time: 10 minutes
Cooking time: 30 minutes
Serves: 4-6

Ⓥ Ingredients

**6 large potatoes, peeled
  and cubed**
4 tablespoons (60 ml) butter
⅓ cup (80 ml) cream
salt and pepper to taste
pinch nutmeg (optional)

1. Put the potatoes in a large pot and cover with water. Bring to a boil and cook until potatoes are soft and ready to mash, about 20 minutes. Drain water and allow potatoes to cool slightly.
2. Heat the butter and cream together on the stove top. Add to the potatoes. Mash until smooth and creamy.
3. Season with salt, pepper and nutmeg (if using).

Boerewors meatballs in ushatini tomato sauce

Boerewors is the quintessential South African sausage, so flavourful and spiced just right – which is why it's great to use to make meatballs. And what better accompaniment than our favourite ushatini sauce? The two make the best midweek supper – uncomplicated deliciousness.

Prep time: 15 minutes
Cooking time: 40 minutes
Serves: 4

Ingredients

600 g boerewors
2 tablespoons (30 ml)
olive oil
1 onion, chopped
1 teaspoon (5 ml) minced
garlic
1 teaspoon (5 ml) minced
ginger
½ teaspoon (2½ ml)
turmeric
1 tablespoon (15 ml) curry
powder
2 or 3 tomatoes, grated
1 tablespoon (15 ml) sugar
¼ cup (60 ml) water
salt and pepper to taste
½ cup (125 ml) coconut milk

1. Remove the boerewors meat from its casing and shape into 8-10 equal-sized balls.
2. Heat 1 tablespoon (15 ml) oil on medium heat and fry the meatballs till brown, about 10 minutes. Remove from pan and set aside.
3. Add remaining oil to pan, and fry the onion, garlic and ginger for 1 minute. Add the turmeric and curry powder and cook till fragrant, 2-3 minutes.
4. Add the tomatoes, sugar and water, and simmer for 15 minutes. Season with salt and pepper, then cook for another 10 minutes to thicken.
5. Put the meatballs back into the pan.
6. Add the coconut milk and simmer for 5 minutes.

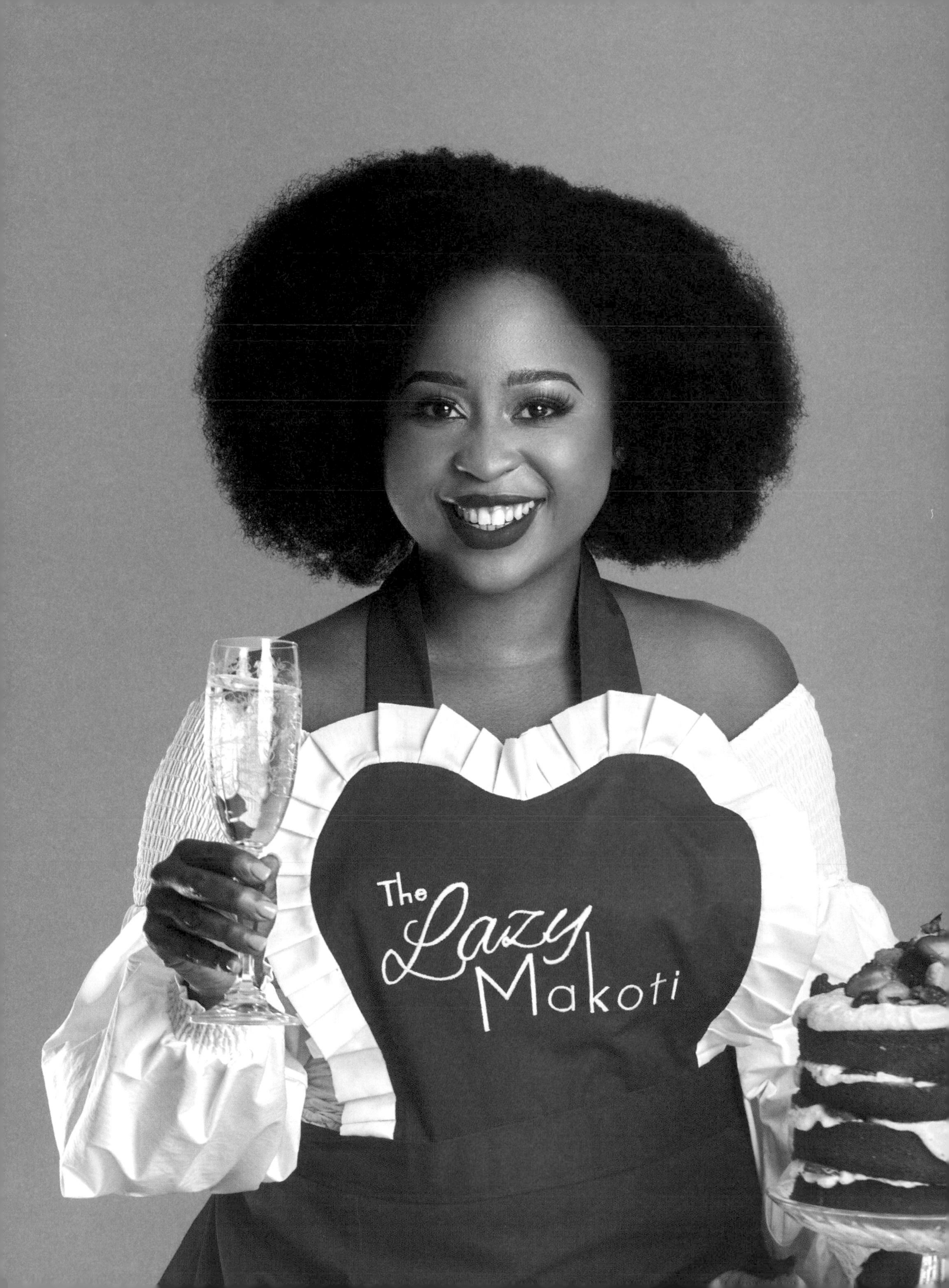
The Lazy Makoti

3

Weekend special

Delicious recipes for a relaxed
weekend of hosting, sport
watching and braaiing.

Spatchcocked peri-peri chicken

Prep time: 10 minutes plus overnight
Cooking time: 20 minutes plus 50 minutes
Serves: 4-6

Ingredients

**2 red peppers, halved and
   deseeded**
1 red onion, chopped
6 cloves garlic, minced
**4-8 red chillies, chopped
   (optional; remove seeds
   to reduce heat if desired)**
**2 tablespoons (30 ml)
   smoked paprika**
1 teaspoon (5 ml) cumin
1 teaspoon (5 ml) lemon juice
**3 tablespoons (45 ml)
   olive oil**
salt and pepper to taste
1 whole chicken

1. Preheat oven to 180 °C.
2. Put the peppers, onion, garlic and chillies (if using) in a roasting pan. Season with spices and drizzle with the lemon juice and olive oil. Add salt and pepper to taste.
3. Roast for 20 minutes till soft. Allow to cool before blending into a peri-peri paste.
4. To spatchcock the chicken, place it breast down on a kitchen surface. Use scissors to cut away either side of the backbone and discard the bone. Use the heel of your hand to open out and flatten the chicken by pressing down.
5. Spread the peri-peri paste over both sides of the chicken. Cover and leave in the fridge for a few hours or overnight.
6. Preheat oven to 180 °C. Place the chicken on baking tray and roast till cooked through, 45-50 minutes – the juices should run clear when a knife is inserted into the thigh.

Seafood boil

This recipe (illustrated on the previous page) has been highly requested on social media – it's safe to say we've all been watching a lot of mukbangs online! A popular American dish, it's made with a variety of seafood and lots of butter, although I've adjusted the butter in this version to a smaller quantity. Feel free to use any seafood that's available to you. This dish is essentially a two-step one: first, boiling the seafood and vegetables, then making the sauce. I assure you, it's well worth the effort!

Prep time: 20 minutes
Cooking time: 30 minutes
Serves: 6-8

Ingredients

6-8 baby potatoes
3 cups (750 ml) water
2 tablespoons (30 ml) cajun spice
2 tablespoons (30 ml) smoked paprika
2 tablespoons (30 ml) garlic powder
2 tablespoons (30 ml) oregano
2 tablespoons (30 ml) onion powder
2 tablespoons (30 ml) lemon and herb seasoning
2 tablespoons (30 ml) cayenne pepper (optional)

1. Place the potatoes in a large pot with the water. Bring to a boil and cook for 5 minutes to soften slightly.
2. Remove from the heat and add the spices and herbs, fish stock and sweetcorn. Return to heat and cook for 5 minutes.
3. Add the seafood, beginning with the items that need the longest cooking: allow 7 minutes for the lobster tails, 5-7 minutes for the mussels and 5 minutes for the prawns.
4. Strain, reserving the cooking liquid, and set the veggies and seafood aside.

1½ cups (375 ml) fish or chicken stock

4 sweetcorn on the cob, halved

4 lobster tails

300 g mussels

8-10 prawns, deveined

For the sauce:

½ cup (125 ml) butter

1 onion, chopped

1 teaspoon (5 ml) minced fresh garlic

2 tablespoons (30 ml) cajun spice

2 tablespoons (30 ml) oregano

2 tablespoons (30 ml) lemon and herb seasoning

1 tablespoon (15 ml) smoked paprika

juice of 1 lemon

5. To make the sauce, melt 2 tablespoons (30 ml) of the butter in a large pan, and fry the onion and garlic till soft, 2-3 minutes. Add the spices and herbs, and cook till fragrant, 3-5 minutes.
6. Add the rest of the butter and allow to melt. Pour in 1-2 cups (250-500 ml) of the reserved liquid.
7. Add the fresh lemon juice and stir well.
8. Add the seafood and veggies to the sauce. Toss well to coat.

Pigs in a blanket with monkeygland sauce

**Prep time: 15 minutes plus 15 minutes in the fridge
Baking time: 20 minutes
Makes: 16**

Ingredients
**1 packet readymade puff
   pastry**
flour for rolling
16 mini pork sausages
1 egg, beaten

For the monkeygland sauce:
**4 tablespoons (60 ml)
   chutney**
**4 tablespoons (60 ml)
   tomato sauce**
**1 tablespoon (15 ml)
   Worcestershire sauce**
**1 teaspoon (5 ml) brown
   sugar**
**1 teaspoon (5 ml) Tabasco
   sauce**

1. Unroll the puff pastry on a lightly floured surface. Use a rolling pin to even it out. Cut the pastry in half lengthwise, then cut each half into eight triangles.
2. Place a sausage on the bottom (wide end) of each triangle, then roll up.
3. Place the pastry-encased sausages seam side down on a greased baking tray. Brush with egg and refrigerate for 15 minutes. Meanwhile, preheat oven to 180 ˚C.
4. Bake until puffed and golden, about 20 minutes, rotating tray halfway through.
5. To make the sauce, combine all the ingredients in a pot and heat to a simmer over medium heat.
6. Serve the pastries warm, with the sauce.

Bunny chow

Prep time: 10 minutes
Cooking time: 40 minutes
Makes: 2

Ingredients
2 tablespoons (30 ml) oil
1 onion, chopped
1 teaspoon (5 ml) minced garlic
1 tablespoon (15 ml) cumin
1 tablespoon (15 ml) curry
  powder
500 g stewing lamb
2 tomatoes, grated
¼ cup (60 ml) water
salt and pepper to taste
chilli to taste (optional)
1 loaf white bread, cut in half
coriander to garnish

1. Heat the oil on medium heat and fry the onion and garlic for 1 minute. Add the cumin and curry powder and fry until fragrant, about 1 minute.
2. Add the lamb and toss to coat. Fry to brown, about 5 minutes.
3. Add the tomatoes and water. Cover and cook till lamb is tender, about 30 minutes.
4. Season with salt and pepper and add chilli if using.
5. Simmer uncovered for 10 minutes to thicken the sauce.
6. In the meantime, hollow out the bread using a knife or your hands to make a well for the curry.
7. Generously spoon in the curry and garnish with coriander.

Salsa

Prep time: 10 minutes
Serves: 2

Ingredients
½ cucumber, cubed
3 tomatoes, cubed
1 red onion, finely chopped
2 tablespoons (30 ml) lemon
  juice
handful chopped coriander
salt and pepper to taste

1. Place all the ingredients in a large bowl and mix well to combine.

Amarula ice-cream cocktail

Prep time: 10 minutes
Serves: 2

Ⓥ Ingredients

**2 cups (500 ml) vanilla
ice cream**
**½ cup (125 ml) Amarula
liqueur**
½ cup (125 ml) cream or milk
grated chocolate to garnish

1. Place the ice cream, liqueur and cream or milk in a blender. Blend briefly to combine.
2. Divide between two cocktail glasses and garnish with chocolate.

WEEKEND SPECIAL

Boozy berry ice lollies

Prep time: 15 minutes plus 6-7 hours in the freezer
Makes: 8

Ⓥ Ingredients

2 cups (500 ml) sparkling wine
¾ cup (190 ml) apple juice
½ cup (125 ml) strawberries, quartered
½ cup (125 ml) blueberries

1. Combine the sparkling wine and apple juice, and fill 8 lolly moulds three-quarters of the way to the top.
2. Add the berries.
3. Put in freezer for 1 hour until lollies begin to harden, then push a lolly stick into each partially frozen lolly. Freeze for 2 hours.
4. Top up with the rest of the sparkling wine and apple juice, and freeze for 3-4 hours.

Easy sweet and savoury snack board

I constantly get asked how to make a cheese/charcuterie board. This is my simple answer. Use any of the following ingredients that are most accessible to you, and enjoy with a glass of South African wine or Méthode Cap Classique – we make some of the best!

Prep time: 20 minutes
Serves: 6

Ingredients

selection of soft cheeses (Camembert, goats' cheese)
selection of aged/firm cheeses (Cheddar, Gouda)
selection of blue cheeses (Gorgonzola)
selection of biltong and cured meats
selection of savoury snacks (olives, gherkins, nuts)
selection of sweet snacks (fresh and dried fruit, preserves, chocolate)
bread sticks and crackers

1. Arrange the cheeses attractively on a large round or rectangular wooden board. Add the meats. Add the savoury snacks. Add the sweet snacks.
2. Add the bread sticks and crackers.

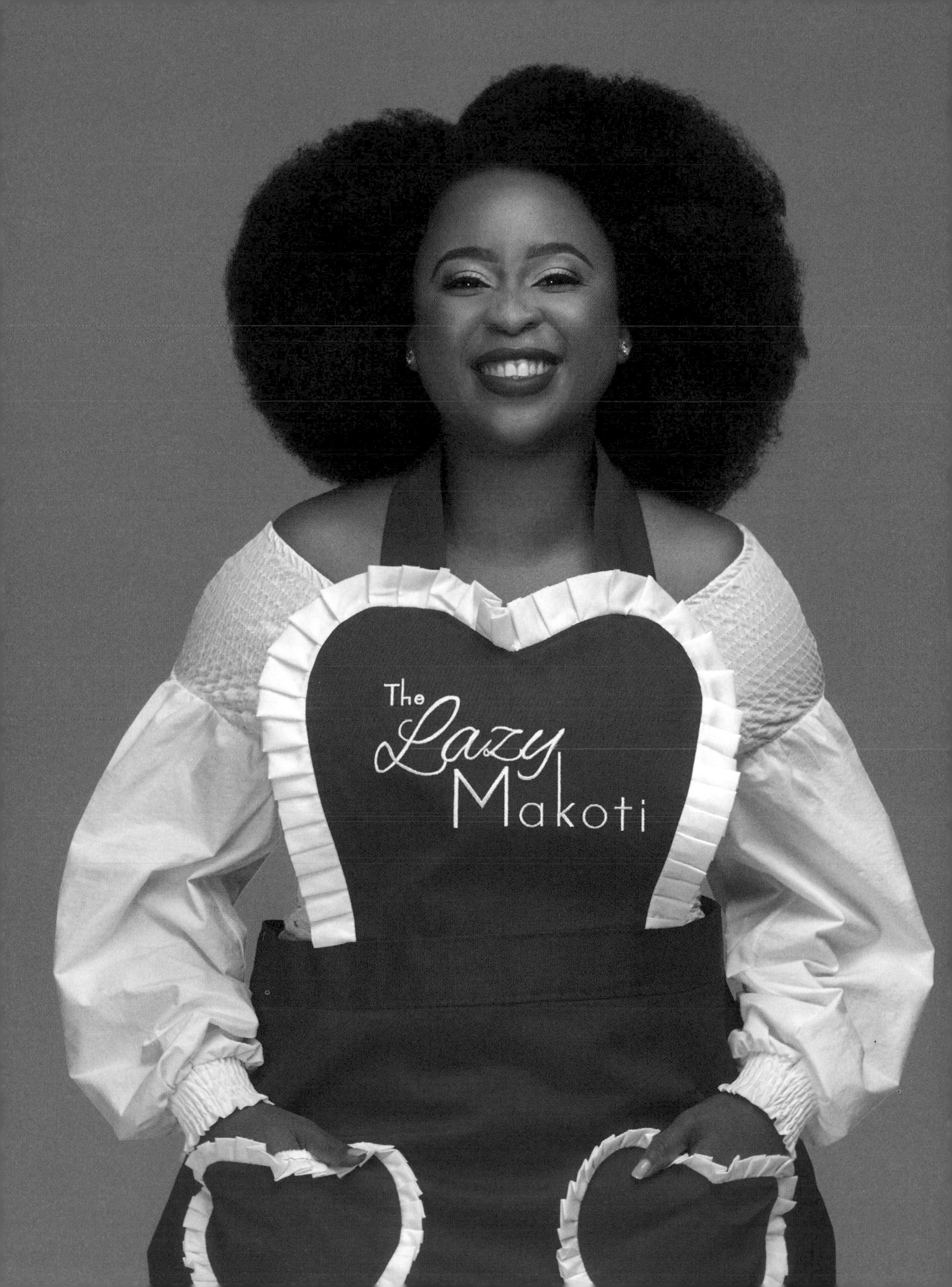
The Lazy Makoti

4

Soul warmers

Essential on chilly winter days –
soups and stews to warm the body
and soul.

Immune booster

When Covid hit, with it came a renewed consciousness of taking care of our bodies. Never has 'your health is your wealth' been more understood by this generation. This is one of my mom's recipes that she used to make for us in flu season, and boy did we have lots of it this past year! So for that extra boost, try this.

Prep time: 10 minutes
Cooking time: 10 minutes
Makes: 2 servings of ½ cup each

Ⓥ Ingredients

1 tablespoon (15 ml) honey
juice of 2 lemons
1 cup (250 ml) orange juice
2 cloves garlic, minced
1 teaspoon (5 ml) freshly
  grated ginger
¼ teaspoon (generous
  pinch) cayenne pepper
¼ teaspoon (generous
  pinch) turmeric

1. Put all the ingredients in a saucepan over medium heat and stir to combine. Once the honey has dissolved, turn off the heat and leave to cool. Can be served warm or cold.

Beef bone broth

The benefits of a good bone broth really are endless, from supporting immune function to aiding good digestion. I make a big batch and allow it to cook slowly for hours on end, filling the house with an amazing aroma of warmth. I then store it in batches in the freezer, to defrost as and when I need it. It can be served as a warming broth, and it's also great to add to stews and soups for extra flavour, the way you would add stock.

Prep time: 15 minutes plus 20 minutes resting
Cooking time: 30 minutes plus 8 hours
Makes: 1 litre

Ingredients

1½ kg beef bones
2 tablespoons (30 ml) olive oil
1 tablespoon (15 ml) apple cider vinegar
1 onion, roughly chopped
2 cloves garlic, chopped
1 teaspoon (5 ml) chopped ginger
2 carrots, peeled and chopped
2 stalks celery, chopped (optional)
salt and pepper to taste

1. Preheat oven to 200 °C.
2. Lay the bones on a baking tray and drizzle with olive oil. Roast for 30 minutes.
3. Put the roasted bones in a large pot with the apple cider vinegar and enough water to cover. Leave to rest for 20 minutes.
4. Add the vegetables. Season well with salt and pepper.
5. Bring to a boil, then reduce heat and simmer on lowest heat for 8 hours, topping up the water when necessary. Skim off any foam that collects on the surface from time to time. The broth is done when it is a rich golden-brown colour, and any meat is falling off the bones.
6. Strain into a container. Discard the bones and vegetables.
7. Leave to cool completely. Store in portions in the freezer.

Chicken and rice soup

This is one of my favourite soups to make – it's simple, delicious and inexpensive. The rice makes it more satisfying and filling – it really is a bowl of goodness. It's also easily adaptable – instead of using the rice to bulk up the soup, you can use any grain, such as barley or lentils.

Prep time: 15 minutes
Cooking time: 40 minutes
Serves: 4-6

Ingredients

2 chicken breasts

salt and pepper to taste

2 tablespoons (30 ml) olive oil

1 onion, diced

1 teaspoon (5 ml) minced garlic

2 carrots, peeled and chopped

1 cup (250 ml) long-grain rice

4 cups (1 litre) chicken stock

1 bay leaf

finely chopped parsley or coriander to garnish

1. Season the chicken breasts on both sides with salt and pepper.
2. In a large pot, heat 1 tablespoon (15 ml) oil and cook the chicken for 4-5 minutes on each side. Remove from pot and set aside.
3. Add the rest of the oil to the same pan, and fry the onion, garlic and carrots until the onion is translucent, 2-3 minutes.
4. Add the rice, stir and cook for 1 minute to lightly toast the grains.
5. Add the chicken breasts, chicken stock and bay leaf. Bring to the boil, then reduce heat and simmer, covered, until rice is tender and chicken is cooked, about 20 minutes.
6. Remove the chicken and bay leaf from the pot. Once the chicken is cool enough to handle, shred it, then put it back into the soup. (The rice may absorb liquid as it sits, so add more stock if needed.)
7. Taste and adjust seasoning. Garnish with parsley or coriander.

Veggie soup

The perfect 'just before month end' soup. Great to clean up your fridge – you can chuck almost any vegetable into this to make a delicious, rich soup that can be enjoyed with bread. And leftovers can be frozen in batches for next time.

**Prep time: 15 minutes
Cooking time: 35 minutes
Serves: 4**

Ⓥ Ingredients

2 tablespoons (30 ml) oil
1 onion, chopped
1 teaspoon (5 ml) minced garlic
½ teaspoon (2½ ml) minced ginger
1 teaspoon (5 ml) turmeric
1 teaspoon (5 ml) curry powder
3 cups chopped vegetables (potato, butternut, carrot, corn, tomato)
2 cups (500 ml) water or vegetable stock
1 cup (250 ml) cream or coconut cream
salt and pepper to taste
finely chopped coriander to garnish
croutons to garnish (optional)

1. Heat the oil in a saucepan on medium heat, then add the onion and fry for 1 minute to soften.
2. Add the garlic, ginger, turmeric and curry powder, and fry till fragrant, 2-3 minutes.
3. Add the vegetables and water or stock. Cook till the vegetables are soft, about 30 minutes. (Top up water while cooking if necessary.)
4. For a smooth soup, leave to cool slightly, then blend (reheat again before serving). For a chunkier soup, don't blend.
5. Add cream or coconut cream and seasoning, and garnish with coriander, and croutons if using.

Pea soup

Prep time: 15 minutes
Cooking time: 30 minutes
Serves: 4

Ingredients

2 tablespoons (30 ml) oil
1 onion, finely chopped
1 teaspoon (5 ml) minced garlic
1 teaspoon (5 ml) minced ginger
few sprigs fresh thyme
1 large potato, peeled and cubed
3 cups (750 ml) frozen peas
2 cups (500 ml) chicken stock
2 tablespoons (30 ml) finely chopped coriander
2 tablespoons (30 ml) cream cheese
salt and pepper to taste
fresh cream to garnish

1. Heat the oil in a medium pot and fry the onion, garlic, ginger and thyme for 2-3 minutes.
2. Add the potato, peas and stock, and cook till the potato is soft, about 20 minutes.
3. Add the coriander and cream cheese. Season with salt and pepper. Remove from heat and allow to cool.
4. Blend till smooth.
5. Reheat, and serve garnished with a swirl of fresh cream. (Illustrated on previous page.)

Curried cream of corn soup

Prep time: 10 minutes
Cooking time: 25 minutes
Serves: 4-6

Ingredients

**2 tablespoons (30 ml)
olive oil**
1 onion, chopped
**2 tablespoons (30 ml) curry
powder**
**2 tins whole-kernel
sweetcorn**
1 cup (250 ml) chicken stock
salt and pepper to taste
**1 cup (250 ml) fresh cream
or evaporated milk**

1. Heat the oil in a pan. Fry the onion for 1 minute, then add the curry powder and sauté till fragrant, 2-3 minutes.
2. Add the sweetcorn with its brine and the stock. Simmer for 20 minutes. Season with salt and pepper.
3. Leave to cool completely, then blend till smooth.
4. Reheat, then add cream or evaporated milk.
5. Serve hot. (Illustrated on previous page.)

Goat and cabbage stew

Goat meat when cooked right can be the most delicious thing you've ever tasted.

Prep time: 15 minutes
Cooking time: 1½ hours
Serves: 6

Ingredients

600 g goat meat
salt and pepper to taste
2 tablespoons (30 ml) oil
1 onion, chopped
1 teaspoon (5 ml) minced garlic
1 teaspoon (5 ml) minced ginger
2 teaspoons (10 ml) curry powder
1 teaspoon (5 ml) paprika
1 beef stock cube
1 teaspoon (5 ml) dried mixed herbs
1 cup (250 ml) water
2 tablespoons (30 ml) Worcestershire sauce
1½ cups (375 ml) shredded cabbage

1. Season the meat with salt and pepper. Heat 1 tablespoon (15 ml) oil, and fry meat to brown, about 10 minutes. Remove from pot and set aside.
2. Add rest of oil to same pot and, over medium heat, fry the onion, garlic, ginger, curry powder and paprika for 2 minutes.
3. Return the goat meat to the pot. Crumble in the stock cube and add the mixed herbs. Toss to coat the meat, then fry for 5 minutes.
4. Add the water and Worcestershire sauce. Bring to a simmer and cook until meat is tender, about 1 hour.
5. Add the cabbage and cook for a further 15 minutes.
6. Serve with hot pap.

Samp and lamb bones

Prep time: 15 minutes plus overnight
Cooking time: 3 hours
Serves: 4-6

Ingredients

2 cups (500 ml) dried samp and beans, soaked overnight and drained
3 cups (750 ml) cold water
2 tablespoons (30 ml) olive oil
500 g meaty lamb bones
1 onion, finely chopped
1 teaspoon (5 ml) minced garlic
1 teaspoon (5 ml) curry powder
½ teaspoon (2½ ml) turmeric
1 teaspoon (5 ml) barbecue spice
1 tomato, grated
1 large potato, peeled and cubed
½ beef stock cube
1 sprig thyme
1 bay leaf

1. Place the samp and beans in a large pot with 2½ cups (625 ml) water. Boil until cooked, about 1½ hours. Do not drain water.
2. In the meantime, heat the oil in another pot and brown the bones for 10 minutes.
3. Add the onion, garlic, curry powder, turmeric and barbecue spice, and sauté until fragrant, 2-3 minutes.
4. Add the samp and beans together with any remaining cooking water, the tomato, potato and crumbled stock cube, plus ½ cup (125 ml) water, and simmer for 30 minutes.
5. Add thyme and bay leaf, and simmer for 10 minutes. Serve warm.

5
Eat more plants

Delicious vegetarian and vegan recipes that are just as tasty as their meat-based counterparts, perfect for Veganuary.

Oat milk

I love oat milk as it's easy to make and even easier on the pocket. Best of all, you only need two ingredients: oats and water.

Prep time: 15 minutes
Makes: 1 litre

(V) Ingredients
1 cup rolled oats
4 cups (1 litre) cold water

1. Put the oats and water in a blender. Blend on high speed for 30 seconds (any longer will make it slimy).
2. Sieve the mixture through a muslin cloth, then strain it again.
3. Transfer to a sealed container and refrigerate. It keeps for 3-4 days. Shake before serving.

Tip: Add flavour with ½ teaspoon (2½ ml) vanilla essence and a pinch of salt.

Dunked cauliflower

Prep time: 15 minutes
Cooking time: 30 minutes
Serves: 4-6

Ingredients

1 large head cauliflower
1½ cups (375 ml) amasi or
   plain yoghurt
¼ cup (60 ml) sriracha
   sauce or other hot sauce
1½ cups (375 ml) flour
1 teaspoon (5 ml) garlic
   powder
2 teaspoons (10 ml) paprika
1 teaspoon (5 ml) chicken
   spice
½ teaspoon (2½ ml) black
   pepper
1 tablespoon (15 ml) dried
   mixed herbs
oil for deep-frying
½ cup (125 ml) mayo
finely chopped herbs
   (parsley, thyme, chives)

For the dunking sauce:

½ cup (125 ml) honey
½ cup (125 ml) soy sauce
¼ cup (60 ml) hot sauce

1. Wash the cauliflower head under running water. Shake off water and cut into bite-sized florets.
2. In a medium-sized bowl, combine the amasi, hot sauce and ¼ cup (60 ml) flour.
3. In a separate bowl, combine the spices, herbs and the rest of the flour.
4. Dip the cauliflower florets in the amasi mixture to coat completely, then dip in the flour mixture to coat completely. Repeat this, dipping each floret first in the amasi mixture and then in the flour, ensuring it's completely coated.
5. Over medium heat, heat enough oil to deep-fry. Deep-fry cauliflower florets in batches and drain on paper towel.
6. Combine dunking sauce ingredients. Dunk each fried floret and transfer to a serving dish.
7. Combine mayo and herbs in a separate bowl. Serve dunked florets warm, with the herb-mayo dip on the side.

Lentil cottage pie

Prep time: 10 minutes
Cooking time: 40 minutes
Serves: 6

Ⓥ Ingredients

**2 tablespoons (30 ml)
  olive oil**
1 onion, chopped
**2 teaspoons (10 ml) minced
  garlic**
2 teaspoons (10 ml) cumin
1 teaspoon (5 ml) turmeric
**1 cup (250 ml) chopped
  spinach or cabbage**
salt and pepper to taste
1 tin lentils, drained
**¼ cup (60 ml) vegetable
  stock**
**The perfect mash (recipe on
  page 39)**

1. In a large pot, heat the oil and fry the onion and garlic for about 1 minute.
2. Add the cumin and turmeric and fry till fragrant, about 2 minutes.
3. Add the spinach or cabbage and cook till wilted, about 5 minutes. Season with salt and pepper.
4. Add the lentils and stock, and combine well. Cook for 5-10 minutes.
5. Preheat oven to 180 °C.
6. Pour the lentil mixture into a baking dish. Spread The perfect mash over the top, then use a fork to make decorative patterns in the mash.
7. Bake till golden and bubbling, about 20 minutes.

Cauliflower 'mac' and cheese

Of course, there's no macaroni in this recipe but it's perfect for days when you crave actual mac and cheese but would rather not have the extra calories. Cauliflower makes a great replacement here and the cheesy goodness of this recipe will leave you wanting more!

Prep time: 10 minutes
Cooking time: 25 minutes
Serves: 4-6

 ## Ingredients

2 cauliflower heads, cut into florets
¼ cup (60 ml) water
2 tablespoons (30 ml) butter
3 tablespoons (45 ml) flour
1½ cups (375 ml) milk
salt and pepper to taste
1 cup (250 ml) grated cheese (half Cheddar, half Gouda)

1. Preheat oven to 180 °C.
2. Put the cauliflower and water in a saucepan. Bring to a boil and cook on medium heat for 5-8 minutes. Drain and set aside.
3. In another pan, melt the butter. Stir in the flour and cook for 2-4 minutes. Add the milk gradually while whisking, and continue whisking till thickened, 5-8 minutes. Season with salt and pepper.
4. Remove from heat. Add the cheese and stir to melt.
5. Put the cauliflower florets into the cheese sauce and toss to coat. Pour everything into a baking dish.
6. Bake for 15 minutes till golden and bubbly, then grill for 2 minutes till top is slightly browned.

Ultimate veggie burger

Prep time: 15 minutes
Cooking time: 30 minutes
Serves: 6

Ⓥ Ingredients

- **3 tablespoons (45 ml) olive oil**
- **½ onion, finely chopped**
- **1 teaspoon (5 ml) minced garlic**
- **1 teaspoon (5 ml) turmeric**
- **1 carrot, grated**
- **½ cup (125 ml) finely chopped spinach**
- **½ tin chickpeas, mashed (reserve half the brine)**
- **salt and pepper to taste**
- **1 tin cooked lentils, mashed**
- **1 cooked sweet potato, mashed**
- **6 burger buns**
- **½ cup (125 ml) mayo**
- **lettuce, tomato, red onion, pesto for assembling**

1. Heat 2 tablespoons (30 ml) oil in a pan. Add the onion and garlic, and fry on medium heat until soft, about 2 minutes. Add the turmeric and fry until fragrant, 1-2 minutes.
2. Add the carrot and spinach, along with the reserved chickpea brine. Season with salt and pepper and simmer till done, about 15 minutes.
3. Add the chickpeas, lentils and sweet potato, and mix well to combine.
4. Preheat oven to 180 ˚C. Grease a baking tray.
5. Using your hands, shape the mixture into 6 burger patties.
6. Place on baking tray, brush with oil on each side and bake for 12 minutes, turning halfway through.
7. Spread both halves of each bun with mayo. Assemble burgers, layering each patty with lettuce, tomato, onion and pesto.

Sorghum rainbow salad

Sorghum is a proudly South African ingredient that's loved by many. Most of us have had it in ting and mqombhothi, but I bet you didn't know that, much like couscous, you can include it in salads as well. Try this.

Prep time: 15 minutes plus overnight
Cooking time: 40 minutes
Serves: 4

(V) **Ingredients**

1 cup (250 ml) sorghum, soaked overnight, then drained

3 cups (750 ml) water

1 cup (250 ml) cherry tomatoes

1 feta round, crumbled

1 red onion, finely chopped

½ cucumber, chopped

1 cup (250 ml) finely chopped herbs (parsley, chives, dill)

salt and pepper to taste

1. In a medium pot, cook the sorghum in the water till soft, about 40 minutes. Drain and leave to cool.
2. Place the sorghum in a large bowl, along with the tomatoes, feta, onion, cucumber and herbs.
3. Season well and toss to combine.

Three-bean curry

A twist on the classic three-bean salad we all grew up loving.

Prep time: 10 minutes
Cooking time: 30 minutes
Serves: 4-6

Ⓥ Ingredients

2 tablespoons (30 ml) oil
1 onion, chopped
1 teaspoon (5 ml) minced ginger
1 teaspoon (5 ml) minced garlic
2 teaspoons (10 ml) curry powder
½ teaspoon (2½ ml) turmeric
2 tomatoes, grated
1 teaspoon (5 ml) sugar
¼ cup (60 ml) water
salt and pepper to taste
¼ cup (60 ml) coconut milk
1 tin butterbeans, drained
1 tin kidney beans, drained
1 tin black beans, drained
coriander to garnish

1. Heat the oil in a pot and fry the onion on medium heat for 1 minute. Add the ginger, garlic, curry powder and turmeric, and fry till fragrant, 2-3 minutes.
2. Add the tomatoes, sugar and water. Simmer for 20 minutes. Season with salt and pepper.
3. Stir in the coconut milk and combine well.
4. Add the beans. Simmer, uncovered, for 5 minutes.
5. Garnish with chopped coriander and serve with Easy flatbread (recipe on page 30).

Avo, corn and feta salad

Prep time: 10 minutes
Serves: 4

(V) Ingredients

2 or 3 avocados, diced

1 red onion, finely chopped

½ cucumber, chopped

1 feta round, crumbled

**1 cup (250 ml) halved cherry
   tomatoes**

**1 tin whole-kernel corn,
   drained**

juice of 1 lemon

salt and pepper to taste

1. Combine the avo, onion, cucumber, feta, cherry tomatoes and corn in a bowl.
2. Sprinkle with the lemon juice and season with salt and pepper. Serve immediately.

Kiwi and cucumber salad

Prep time: 10 minutes
Serves: 4

Ⓥ Ingredients

2 or 3 kiwifruit, peeled and
sliced
2 cups (500 ml) rocket
1 feta round, cubed
½ small red onion, finely
chopped
½ cucumber, sliced

For the dressing:
¼ cup (60 ml) olive oil
juice and zest of 1 lemon
2 teaspoons (10 ml) honey
1 tablespoon (15 ml) vinegar
salt and pepper to taste

1. Combine the salad ingredients in a large bowl, as illustrated on previous page.
2. Combine the dressing ingredients and mix well.
3. Dress the salad and toss to coat.

Cauli rice

Prep time: 10 minutes
Cooking time: 6 minutes
Serves: 2-4

Ⓥ Ingredients

1 large head cauliflower
1 tablespoon (15 ml) olive oil
salt and pepper to taste
1 teaspoon (5 ml) turmeric
  (optional)

1. Dry the cauliflower thoroughly. Chop it into large pieces. Pulse it in a food processor or grate it.
2. Heat the oil over medium heat. Add the cauli rice and sauté for 1 minute. Cover with a lid and steam for 5 minutes.
3. Season with salt and pepper, and add turmeric for colour if desired. (Illustrated on next page.)

Roasted butternut and chickpea curry

Prep time: 10 minutes
Cooking time: 55 minutes
Serves: 4

 Ingredients

1 butternut, peeled and cubed, or 300 g pre-prepared butternut cubes
¼ cup (60 ml) olive oil
salt and pepper to taste
1 onion, chopped
1 teaspoon (5 ml) fresh minced ginger
1 teaspoon (5 ml) minced garlic
1 teaspoon (5 ml) turmeric
2 teaspoons (10 ml) cumin
1 tomato, grated
¼ cup (60 ml) water
1 tin chickpeas, drained
½ tin coconut milk
fresh coriander to garnish

1. Preheat oven to 180 °C.
2. Place the butternut on a baking tray and drizzle with 2 tablespoons (30 ml) olive oil. Season with salt and pepper. Roast till tender, about 30 minutes.
3. In the meantime, heat the remaining olive oil in a saucepan. Add the onion and sauté for 1 minute. Add the ginger, garlic and spices, and fry till fragrant, 2-3 minutes.
4. Add the tomato and water. Lower heat to a gentle simmer and cook for 15 minutes.
5. Add the chickpeas and roasted butternut, and stir to coat vegetables.
6. Add the coconut milk and stir to combine.
7. Garnish with coriander and serve with Cauli rice (recipe on previous page).

Vegan chocolate mousse

**Prep time: 20 minutes plus 1 hour in the fridge
Serves: 4**

Ingredients

**200 g dark chocolate,
chopped into pieces
1 cup aquafaba (brine from
tinned chickpeas)
½ cup (125 ml) sugar
strawberries to garnish**

1. Melt the chocolate in a double boiler or a bowl placed over a pot of hot water.
2. In a separate bowl, beat the aquafaba with the sugar till stiff peaks form, about 10 minutes.
3. Gently fold in the melted chocolate.
4. Spoon into serving glasses and chill for at least 1 hour.
5. Garnish with strawberries.

6

Proudly Mzansi

A taste of home – childhood
favourites from Gogo's kitchen.
Traditional South African foods that
celebrate our heritage.

Motepa breakfast porridge

Prep time: 5 minutes plus 1 day for fermenting
Cooking time: 20 minutes
Serves: 6

Ⓥ Ingredients

1 cup (250 ml) maize meal
4 cups (1 litre) water
½ teaspoon (2½ ml) salt
1 tablespoon (15 ml) butter
milk and sugar or honey
to serve

1. Mix maize meal with 1 cup (250 ml) cold water to make a smooth paste. Leave to ferment in a warm spot for 1 day.
2. The next day, bring 3 cups (750 ml) water to the boil in a large pot, and add the salt.
3. Whisk the fermented maize meal into the boiling water, working quickly to break up any lumps. Simmer, covered, until thick and smooth, about 20 minutes.
4. Stir in the butter.
5. Serve with milk and sugar or honey.

Kgodu

I learned this recipe from my grandmother, and I'm reminded of her every time I make it. She used wild melon, which is very similar to butternut or pumpkin, but it's hard to find in the city, so I've used butternut. My other twist is the addition of peanut butter; she always used crushed peanuts. It's nice to find a way to enjoy childhood favourites with a few substitutions.

**Prep time: 10 minutes
Cooking time: 50 minutes
Serves: 6**

Ⓥ Ingredients

**2 cups (500 ml) peeled and cubed pumpkin or butternut
2½ cups (625 ml) water
1 cup (250 ml) maize meal
¼ cup (60 ml) brown sugar
2 tablespoons (30 ml) peanut butter (optional)**

1. Place the pumpkin or butternut and ½ cup (125 ml) water in a pot. Bring to a simmer and cook over medium heat until tender, about 20 minutes. Drain, mash and set aside.
2. In a bowl, combine the maize meal and 1 cup (250 ml) water to form a paste.
3. Bring 1 cup (250 ml) water to boil in a medium-sized pot and add the paste, stirring well to ensure no lumps. Cook, covered, for 10 minutes.
4. Add the mashed pumpkin or butternut and combine well. Cook for a further 15 minutes, stirring occasionally.
5. Sprinkle the sugar over and cook for another 5 minutes.
6. Stir in the peanut butter if desired.

Preserved morogo wa Leroto

Prep time: 10 minutes plus 2 days drying
Cooking time: 20 minutes
Makes: 30 balls

Ⓥ Ingredients

4 cups (1 litre) chopped
morogo
1 cup (250 ml) water
salt and pepper to taste

1. Simmer morogo in water with seasoning till soft, about 20 minutes.
2. Mash slightly and leave to cool completely.
3. Shape into 30 golfball-sized balls. Place on a tray to sun-dry for 2 days.

Sautéed cabbage and spinach

Prep time: 5 minutes
Cooking time: 20 minutes
Serves: 4-6 as a side

Ⓥ Ingredients

2 tablespoons (30 ml) oil
1 onion, finely chopped
1 teaspoon (5 ml) curry
powder
2 carrots, grated
1 cup shredded cabbage
1 cup shredded spinach
salt and pepper to taste

1. Heat the oil and fry the onion for 1 minute. Add the curry powder and fry till fragrant, about 3 minutes.
2. Add the carrot and cabbage and sauté till cooked, about 10 minutes.
3. Add the spinach and cook until wilted, about 5 minutes. Season to taste. (Illustrated on next page.)

Tshohlo

**Prep time: 10 minutes
Cooking time: 3 hours
Serves: 4-6**

Ingredients
**800 g stewing beef, cubed
1 onion, chopped
1½ cups (375 ml) beef stock
1 bay leaf
salt and pepper to taste
1 tablespoon (15 ml) flour**

1. Place the meat, onion, stock and bay leaf in a pot. Bring to a simmer, and cook till beef is tender, 2-3 hours.
2. Season with salt and pepper. Remove bay leaf. Shred the meat.
3. Stir in the flour and cook till thickened, about 5 minutes. Serve with Ting.

Ting

**Prep time: 5 minutes plus overnight for fermenting
Cooking time: 30 minutes
Serves: 6**

(V) Ingredients
**1 cup (250 ml) sorghum
4 cups (1 litre) water
1 cup (250 ml) maize meal**

1. Put sorghum in a plastic container and stir in 1 cup (250 ml) water to form a paste. Seal and leave overnight to ferment.
2. The next day, mix the maize meal into the fermented sorghum.
3. Bring 3 cups (750 ml) water to the boil. Gradually add the sorghum mixture, stirring quickly to break up lumps. Cover, turn heat to low, and cook for 10 minutes.
4. Using a wooden spoon, stir to break up lumps. Cook for a further 10 minutes. Serve warm.

Gizzards

Prep time: 10 minutes
Cooking time: 55 minutes
Serves: 4

Ingredients

2 tablespoons (30 ml) oil
1 onion, chopped
1 teaspoon (5 ml) minced
garlic
1 teaspoon (5 ml) minced
ginger
½ teaspoon (2½ ml) cumin
½ teaspoon (2½ ml)
cayenne pepper
½ teaspoon (2½ ml) paprika
250 g chicken gizzards,
cleaned
1 cup (250 ml) water
salt and pepper to taste
1 bay leaf
handful chopped coriander

1. In a pan, heat the oil and fry the onion, garlic, ginger and spices till softened, about 2 minutes.
2. Add the gizzards and water, and cook, covered, on medium heat for 45 minutes.
3. Season with salt and pepper. Add the bay leaf.
4. Simmer, uncovered, for 10 minutes to thicken.
5. Add the chopped coriander.

Potbread

Prep time: 20 minutes plus 40 minutes for rising
Baking time: 50 minutes
Makes: 1 loaf

Ⓥ Ingredients

6 cups (1½ litres) cake flour,
** plus extra for kneading**
1 packet instant dry yeast
¼ cup (60 ml) sugar
1 teaspoon (5 ml) salt
2¾ cups (690 ml) warm water
oil for greasing

1. In a large bowl, combine the dry ingredients. Make a well in the centre and pour in the water, stirring. Combine well to form a dough.
2. Knead on a lightly floured surface until elastic, 6-8 minutes.
3. Lightly grease a bowl with oil and place dough in. Cover and leave in a warm spot till doubled in size, about 30 minutes.
4. Light the fire or braai. Grease a large cast-iron pot and the inside of its lid.
5. Knock down the dough by punching it lightly, and shape it into a ball. Place it in the pot and leave to rise, covered, for 10 minutes.
6. Place pot on braai, with a few coals on the lid, and bake for 50 minutes.

7

Sunday kos

Sunday has always meant a seven-colour spread on my family table. On this day we wake up at the crack of dawn to make all our favourites.

Chicken roast

Prep time: 10 minutes
Cooking time: 1 hour, 15 minutes
Serves: 6

Ingredients

1 whole chicken
½ cup (125 ml) butter,
  at room temperature
1 teaspoon (5 ml) paprika
1 teaspoon (5 ml) garlic
  powder
1 teaspoon (5 ml) cumin
1 tablespoon (15 ml) chicken
  spice
¼ cup (60 ml) finely
  chopped fresh herbs
  (parsley, thyme, rosemary)
1 medium onion, halved

1. Pat the chicken dry. Preheat oven to 180 ˚C.
2. In a small bowl, combine the butter, spices and herbs. Mix well.
3. Rub the chicken generously with the butter mixture, including inside the cavity and under the skin. Stuff the cavity with the onion.
4. Place the chicken on a baking tray and roast till golden and cooked through, 1 hour and 15 minutes. Turn once or twice and baste during cooking.

Rice-stuffed fish

Prep time: 15 minutes
Cooking time: 35 minutes
Serves: 6

Ingredients

1 cup (250 ml) rice
2 tablespoons (30 ml) olive oil, plus extra for drizzling
½ onion, finely chopped
1 teaspoon (5ml) minced garlic
½ red pepper, finely chopped
½ green pepper, finely chopped
½ yellow pepper, finely chopped
1 teaspoon (5 ml) turmeric
handful herbs (parsley, dill, coriander)
salt and pepper to taste
1 snoek or yellowtail, cleaned and patted dry
2 lemons, sliced

1. Cook the rice according to the packet directions. Set aside.
2. In a large pot, heat the oil. Fry the onion till translucent, about 1 minute.
3. Add the garlic and peppers, and fry to soften, about 2 minutes.
4. Add the turmeric and fry for about 1 minute.
5. Add the rice and stir well to coat the grains. Add the herbs. Season with salt and pepper.
6. Preheat oven to 180 ˚C. Cover bottom of a baking tray with foil.
7. Using a sharp knife, make 3 incisions on either side of the fish. Season well with salt and pepper inside and outside. Place the fish on the baking tray.
8. Stuff the fish with the rice mixture, then drizzle with olive oil.
9. Push the lemon slices into the incisions on either side of the fish.
10. Bake till the fish is cooked and flaky, about 12 minutes.

Oxtail and bean stew

One of the most requested recipes is for an oxtail stew with no wine. And here it is! This I know you will love.

**Prep time: 15 minutes plus 2 hours or overnight in the fridge
Cooking time: 3 hours
Serves: 6**

Ingredients

1 kg oxtail
2 tablespoons (30 ml) oil
1 onion, chopped
1 teaspoon (5 ml) minced garlic
1 teaspoon (5 ml) minced ginger
2 chillies, chopped (optional)
2 cups (500 ml) beef or chicken stock
1 tablespoon (15 ml) sugar
1 tin butter beans, drained

For the marinade:

6 tablespoons (90 ml) soy sauce
4 tablespoons (60 ml) Worcestershire sauce
1 tablespoon (15 ml) tomato sauce
1 teaspoon (5 ml) garlic powder
1 teaspoon (5 ml) paprika

1. In a bowl, combine the marinade ingredients.
2. Put the oxtail in a large bowl and pour the marinade over. Toss to coat. Leave for at least 2 hours or overnight in the fridge.
3. Heat 1 tablespoon (15 ml) oil in a large pot. Brown the oxtail in batches, removing from pot and setting aside as each batch is browned. Reserve the marinade.
4. Preheat oven to 180 °C. (This can also be cooked, covered, on the stove top at a simmer.)
5. Add 1 tablespoon (15 ml) oil to the pot, then add the onion and fry gently for 2 minutes.
6. Add the garlic and ginger, and the chillies if using.
7. Return the oxtail to the pot. Add the marinade, stock and sugar.
8. Cook till tender, about 3 hours.
9. Add the butter beans and stir to combine.

Potato and tuna salad

Prep time: 5 minutes
Cooking time: 25 minutes
Serves: 6

Ingredients

10-12 baby potatoes
¼ cup (60 ml) mayonnaise
2 tablespoons (30 ml)
  mustard
1 tin shredded tuna, drained
1 small red onion, chopped
handful chopped herbs
  (parsley, chives)
salt and pepper to taste

1. Put the potatoes in a large pot with water to cover. Bring to a boil and cook till the potatoes are tender, about 25 minutes. Drain and leave to cool slightly. Halve each potato.
2. Combine the mayo and mustard in a large bowl. Add the potatoes, tuna, onion and herbs, then season.
3. Toss gently to combine.

Spicy Sunday rice

Prep time: 15 minutes
Cooking time: 30 minutes
Serves: 6-8

(V) Ingredients

**1 cup (250 ml) lentils,
  well rinsed**
2 cups (500 ml) water
1½ cups (375 ml) rice
2 tablespoons (30 ml) oil
1 onion, chopped
**1 teaspoon (5 ml) minced
  garlic**
**1 teaspoon (5 ml) grated
  ginger**
**2 teaspoons (30 ml) curry
  powder**
**¼ teaspoon (generous
  pinch) turmeric**
salt and pepper to taste
**finely chopped herbs to
  garnish (optional)**

1. Put the lentils in a pot with the water. Cook over medium heat till soft, about 25 minutes.
2. In another pot, cook the rice according to the packet directions.
3. Heat the oil in a pan. Fry the onion, garlic and ginger for 1 minute.
4. Add the curry powder and turmeric and fry till fragrant, 2-3 minutes.
5. Combine the curried-onion mixture, lentils and rice. Season with salt and pepper. Mix well.
6. Garnish with chopped herbs if desired.

Garlic-roasted butternut

Prep time: 10 minutes
Cooking time: 40 minutes
Serves: 4

Ⓥ Ingredients

1 butternut, peeled and
roughly chopped
3 tablespoons (45 ml)
olive oil
3 tablespoons (45 ml)
chopped herbs (parsley,
rosemary, thyme, sage)
salt and pepper to taste
1 tablespoon (15 ml) minced
garlic

1. Preheat oven to 200 °C. Grease a baking tray.
2. Place the butternut on the baking tray and drizzle with olive oil.
3. Sprinkle with herbs and season with salt and pepper. Toss to coat evenly. Roast for 20 minutes.
4. Remove from oven and sprinkle with the garlic. Toss to coat. Return to oven and roast till soft, 10-20 minutes.
5. Grill for 2 minutes to brown, keeping a close eye to ensure butternut doesn't burn. Serve hot.

Sunday green medley

Prep time: 10 minutes
Cooking time: 10 minutes
Serves: 6

Ⓥ Ingredients

1 cup (250 ml) long-stem broccoli
1 cup (250 ml) frozen peas
1 cup (250 ml) green beans

For the dressing:
1 tablespoon (15 ml) wholegrain mustard
1 tablespoon (15 ml) balsamic vinegar
1 tablespoon (15 ml) olive oil
1 teaspoon (5 ml) honey
salt and pepper to taste

1. Blanch the veggies by cooking in boiling water for 8 minutes, then immediately rinsing with ice-cold water to stop the cooking process. Transfer to a large bowl.
2. Combine the dressing ingredients and mix well.
3. Pour the dressing over the greens, and toss to coat.

Beetroot and fig salad

Prep time: 15 minutes
Serves: 6

(V) Ingredients

2 cups (500 ml) rocket
**1 cup (250 ml) cooked
cubed beetroot**
3 or 4 figs, quartered
¼ cup (60 ml) walnuts
1 feta round

For the dressing:

**2 tablespoons (30 ml)
olive oil**
**1 tablespoon (15 ml)
balsamic vinegar**
1 tablespoon (15 ml) honey
salt and pepper to taste

1. Wash the rocket well, pat dry and place in a serving bowl.
2. Scatter over the beetroot, figs and nuts. Crumble the feta over.
3. Combine the dressing ingredients and mix well. Drizzle over the salad.

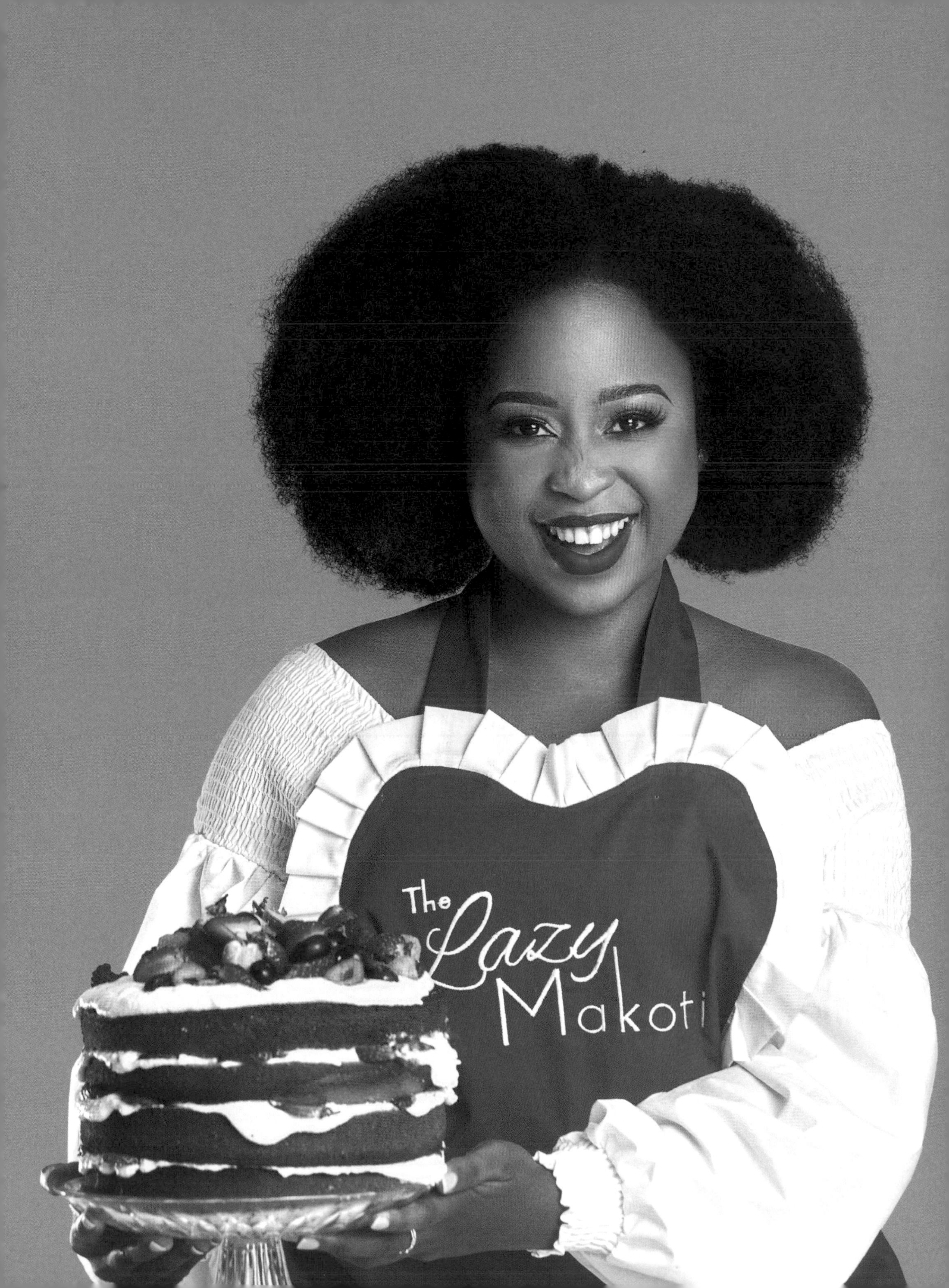
The Lazy Makoti

8

Easy bakes

Everything tastes better
freshly baked.

lemon drizzle loaf

Prep time: 10 minutes
Baking time: 35 minutes
Makes: 1 loaf

Ⓥ Ingredients

3 eggs
1 cup (250 ml) castor sugar
1 cup (250 ml) plain yoghurt
½ cup (125 ml) oil
juice and zest of 2 lemons
1½ cups (375 ml) cake flour
2 teaspoons (10 ml) baking
** powder**
½ teaspoon (2½ ml) salt

For the drizzle:
½ cup (125 ml) icing sugar
4 tablespoons (60 ml)
** lemon juice**

1. Preheat oven to 180 ˚C. Grease a loaf tin.
2. Whisk together the eggs, castor sugar and yoghurt until the sugar is completely dissolved.
3. Add the oil, lemon juice and lemon zest, and combine well.
4. In a separate bowl, combine the flour, baking powder and salt.
5. Mix the dry ingredients into the wet ingredients.
6. Pour into a loaf tin and bake till golden, about 35 minutes. Remove from oven and set aside to cool.
7. To make the drizzle, combine the icing sugar and lemon juice. Drizzle over the cooled loaf.

Easy scones

Prep time: 15 minutes
Baking time: 12 minutes
Makes: 12 scones

 Ingredients

2 cups (500 ml) flour, plus
extra for rolling
1 tablespoon (15 ml) baking
powder
¼ cup (60 ml) sugar
¼ teaspoon (generous
pinch) salt
⅓ cup (80 ml) butter, at room
temperature
1 egg
1 teaspoon (5 ml) vanilla
essence
½ cup (125 ml) milk

1. Preheat oven to 180 °C. Grease a baking tray.
2. Sift the flour and baking powder into a large bowl. Add the sugar and salt, and combine well.
3. Use your fingertips to rub the butter into the dry ingredients until the mixture looks like breadcrumbs.
4. In a separate bowl, whisk together the egg, vanilla essence and milk.
5. Pour the wet ingredients into the dry ingredients, and use your hands to combine.
6. Place the dough on a floured surface. Roll it out using a rolling pin, or press it down using your hands, to a thickness of 2 cm. Cut out scone shapes using a cookie cutter or the rim of a glass.
7. Place on baking tray and bake till golden, 12-15 minutes.

Orange cookies with cream-cheese filling

Prep time: 20 minutes
Baking time: 8 minutes
Makes: 15 biscuits

Ⓥ Ingredients
⅓ cup (80 ml) plain yoghurt
1 teaspoon (5 ml) orange
   zest
1 teaspoon (5 ml)
   bicarbonate of soda
⅓ cup (80 ml) butter
½ cup (125 ml) sugar
1 egg
1¼ cup (315 ml) cake flour
¼ teaspoon (generous
   pinch) salt

For the filling:
1 tub cream cheese
⅓ cup (80 ml) butter,
   at room temperature
¾ cup (190 ml) icing sugar
2 teaspoons (10 ml) orange
   zest

1. Preheat oven to 200 °C. Grease two baking trays.
2. Combine the yoghurt, orange zest and bicarbonate of soda in a large bowl.
3. In a separate bowl, cream the butter and sugar with an electric beater till pale, about 8 minutes.
4. Add the egg and mix well. Pour into the yoghurt mixture.
5. Add the flour and salt. Mix until combined.
6. Spoon into a piping bag, and pipe 30 dollops of mixture onto the baking trays. Alternatively, drop 30 spoonfuls onto the baking trays, using the back of a spoon to shape each biscuit. Leave room between biscuits for spreading.
7. Bake until golden, 5-8 minutes. Remove from oven and carefully transfer onto wire rack to cool completely.
8. Combine filling ingredients and mix well. Use filling to sandwich biscuits together.

Shortbread biscuits

Prep time: 15 minutes
Baking time: 15 minutes
Makes: 16 biscuits

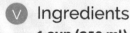 Ingredients

1 cup (250 ml) butter,
at room temperature
½ cup (125 ml) icing sugar
1 teaspoon (5 ml) vanilla
essence
2 cups (500 ml) cake flour,
plus extra for kneading

1. Preheat oven to 180 ˚C. Grease a baking tray.
2. In a large bowl, combine the butter, icing sugar and vanilla essence. Beat until light and fluffy, about 5 minutes.
3. Add the flour. Mix with a wooden spoon until the dough comes together.
4. Gently knead the dough on a lightly floured surface for 2-3 minutes.
5. Roll out to 2 cm thickness and cut into cookies.
6. Place on baking tray and bake until golden, 12-16 minutes. (Illustrated on previous page.)

Easy vanilla sponge

Prep time: 15 minutes
Baking time: 35 minutes
Makes: 2 round cakes

Ⓥ Ingredients

4 eggs
2 cups (500 ml) sugar
1 cup (250 ml) milk
¾ cup (190 ml) oil
1 teaspoon (5 ml) vanilla
**   essence**
2½ cups (625 ml) cake flour
2½ teaspoons (12½ ml)
**   baking powder**

1. Preheat oven to 180 ˚C. Grease two round 23 cm pans.
2. In a large bowl, beat the eggs and sugar together till combined and slightly thickened, about 1 minute.
3. Add the milk, oil and vanilla essence.
4. In a separate bowl, sift the flour and baking powder and combine well.
5. Combine the wet and dry ingredients and mix till just smooth – do not overmix.
6. Pour into prepared pans and bake for 35 minutes or until a skewer inserted comes out clean.
7. Leave to cool completely in tins, then turn onto a rack before icing.

Soft rolls

Prep time: 15 minutes plus 1 hour for rising
Baking time: 12 minutes
Makes: 16 rolls

(V) Ingredients

4 cups (1 litre) flour
1 packet instant dry yeast
⅓ cup (80 ml) castor sugar
1 teaspoon (5 ml) salt
⅓ cup (80 ml) melted
   butter, plus extra for
   brushing
1½ cups (375 ml) warm milk
1 egg
oil for greasing

1. Put 3 cups (750 ml) flour, yeast, castor sugar and salt in a bowl. Combine well.
2. In a separate bowl, mix the butter, milk and egg.
3. Make a well in the centre of the dry ingredients and pour the wet ingredients into it.
4. Add ½ cup (125 ml) flour and combine with a wooden spoon until incorporated.
5. Add the remaining ½ cup (125 ml) flour and mix until a ball of dough is formed.
6. Knead until dough is slightly sticky and soft, and pulling away from sides of bowl, about 8 minutes.
7. Transfer dough to a lightly greased bowl. Cover with a towel or clingwrap, and leave to rise in a warm spot until double in size, about 30 minutes.
8. Knock down dough by punching it lightly. Pinch off pieces and form 16 equal-sized rolls (you can weigh them to ensure consistency), placing them on a greased baking tray.
9. Cover with a towel or clingwrap and leave to rise for 30 minutes. In the meantime, preheat oven to 180 ˚C.
10. Bake until golden, 12-15 minutes. Brush with melted butter while hot.

Homemade white bread

Prep time: 15 minutes plus 40 minutes for rising
Baking time: 30 minutes
Makes: 1 loaf

(V) Ingredients

2 cups (500 ml) white bread
flour
2 teaspoons (10 ml) salt
1 teaspoon (5 ml) sugar
1 packet instant dry yeast
2 tablespoons (30 ml)
melted butter
1¼ cups (315 ml) warm
water, plus extra for
brushing
oil for greasing

1. In a large bowl, combine the flour, salt, sugar and yeast.
2. Add the butter and mix in.
3. Add the water and form into a soft dough. Knead for 6-8 minutes.
4. Put into greased bowl and leave to rise for 10 minutes.
5. Grease a bread tin.
6. Knock down the dough by punching it lightly, then form it into a loaf shape. Place it, seam side down, in the bread tin. Cover with a damp towel and leave to rise till double in size, about 30 minutes.
7. Preheat oven to 180 °C.
8. Brush the top with water and bake for 30 minutes. Leave to cool completely before slicing.

Braided spinach and cheese bread

Prep time: 15 minutes plus 30 minutes for rising
Baking time: 30 minutes
Makes: 1 braid

ⓥ Ingredients

2½ cups (625 ml) cake flour,
plus extra for rolling
1 packet instant dry yeast
1 teaspoon (5 ml) sugar
½ teaspoon (2½ ml) salt
1 cup (250 ml) warm milk
2 tablespoons (30 ml) oil,
plus extra for greasing
and brushing
1 cup (250 ml) finely
chopped spinach
1 teaspoon (5 ml) minced
garlic
½ cup (125 ml) grated
cheese

1. In a large bowl, combine the flour, yeast, sugar and salt.
2. In a separate bowl, combine the milk and oil. Add to dry ingredients. Mix well.
3. Add the spinach and garlic. Combine well.
4. Knead until dough is smooth and elastic, 8-10 minutes. Place in a greased bowl, cover and leave in a warm spot to rise until double in size, about 30 minutes.
5. Preheat oven to 180 °C. Grease a baking tray.
6. Knock down the dough by punching lightly, then roll it out into a rectangle on a floured surface.
7. Sprinkle with the cheese, leaving a 2 cm border all round.
8. Roll up tightly from the longer side. Cut in half lengthwise, then twist the lengths around each other. Brush the top with a little oil.
9. Bake for 30 minutes. Brush with extra oil once baked.

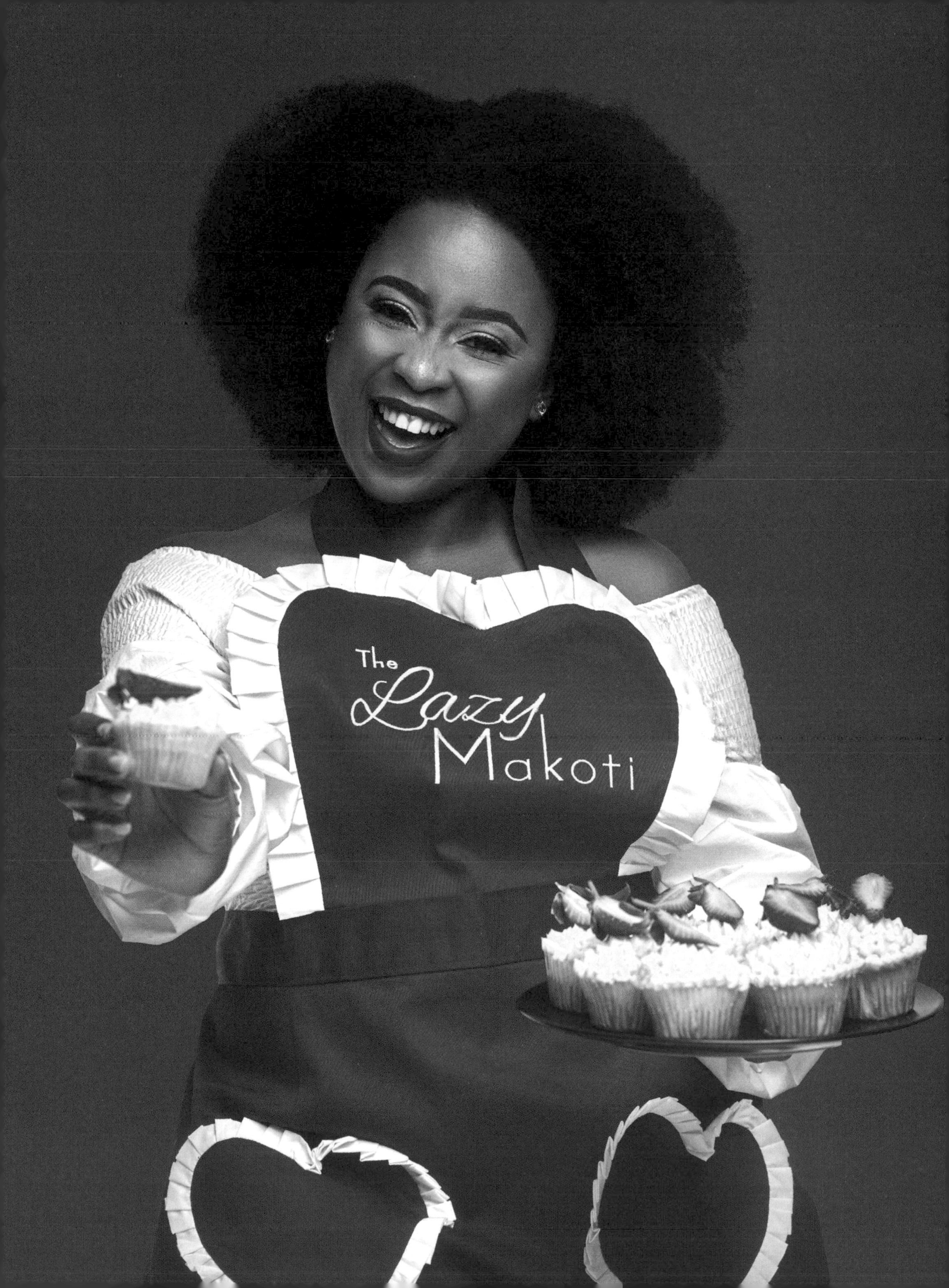
The Lazy Makoti

9
Sweet tooth

Decadent cakes and desserts
to satisfy any sweet tooth.

Layered custard and strawberry cake

Prep time: 20 minutes
Cooking time: 12 minutes
Makes: 1 cake

Ingredients

2 Easy vanilla sponge cakes
   (see page 141)
3 tablespoons (45 ml)
   custard powder
½ cup (125 ml) warm water
1½ cups (375 ml) milk
½ cup (125 ml) butter,
   at room temperature
1 cup (250 ml) castor sugar
1 teaspoon (5 ml) vanilla
   essence
2 cups (500 ml) sliced
   strawberries

1. Cut the 2 cakes in half horizontally, to end up with 4 layers.
2. In a bowl, combine the custard powder with the water to form a smooth paste.
3. Bring the milk to a boil. Stir the custard paste into the boiling milk, and continue stirring until mixture thickens, about 10 minutes.
4. Remove from stove and cover surface with clingwrap to prevent a skin forming. Leave to cool.
5. Beat the butter and castor sugar until light and creamy, about 5 minutes.
6. Add the vanilla essence and cooled custard.
7. Spread a quarter of the custard mixture onto the first layer of cake, and top with sliced strawberries. Repeat with the second and third layers.
8. End with the fourth layer, topped with custard mixture and garnished with strawberries.

Berry swirl cheesecake

**Prep time: 20 minutes plus 5 hours or overnight in the fridge
Cooking time: 30 seconds
Makes: 1 cake**

Ⓥ Ingredients

**1 packet Tennis biscuits
¼ cup (60 ml) melted butter
2 tubs cream cheese
½ cup (125 ml) castor sugar
¼ cup (60 ml) cream
3 tablespoons (45 ml) milk
1½ teaspoons (7½ ml)
   gelatine
½ cup (125 ml) Berry coulis
   (recipe on next page)**

1. Crush the biscuits. Combine with the butter. Pour into the base of a springform pan and smooth with the back of a spoon. Refrigerate while you make the filling.
2. Whip the cream cheese to soften it, about 3 minutes. Add the sugar and combine. Set aside.
3. In a separate bowl, whip the cream till thick, about 5 minutes. Fold it into the cream-cheese mixture.
4. Put the milk in a small bowl, and warm it in the microwave for 30 seconds. Add the gelatine and stir until it has completely dissolved. Pour into the cream-cheese mixture and fold to combine.
5. Remove the biscuit base from the fridge. Pour in the filling and smooth with the back of a spoon or a spatula.
6. Spoon the Berry coulis over the top, and use a skewer to make swirly lines.
7. Refrigerate for 5 hours or overnight.

Berry coulis

Prep time: 10 minutes
Cooking time: 20 minutes
Makes: about 1 cup (250 ml)

Ⓥ Ingredients

2 cups (500 ml) washed and
   chopped mixed berries
½ cup (125 ml) sugar
¼ cup (60 ml) water
2 tablespoons (30 ml) lemon
   juice

1. Put the berries in a small pot. Add the sugar, water and lemon juice.
2. Bring to a simmer over medium heat, stirring until the sugar has dissolved. Simmer for 10 minutes.
3. Mash while warm, or leave to cool, then blend.
4. Return to pot and simmer until thick, about 10 minutes. (Illustrated on previous page.)

Lemon and thyme bundt cake

Prep time: 15 minutes
Baking time: 40 minutes
Makes: 1 cake

Ⓥ Ingredients

3 cups (750 ml) flour

1 tablespoon (15 ml) baking
powder

1 teaspoon (5 ml) salt

2 teaspoons (10 ml) lemon
zest

2 teaspoons (10 ml) finely
chopped thyme

4 large eggs

1½ cups (375 ml) castor
sugar

2 tablespoons (30 ml) lemon
juice

1 cup (250 ml) plain yoghurt

¼ cup (60 ml) milk

1 cup (250 ml) olive oil

edible flowers, curls of
lemon zest and a few
sprigs fresh thyme to
decorate

For the glaze:

1½ cups (375 ml) icing sugar

1 cup (250 ml) plain yoghurt

1. Preheat oven to 180 ˚C. Grease a bundt cake tin.
2. Put the flour, baking powder, salt, lemon zest and thyme in a large bowl. Mix to combine.
3. In a separate bowl, whisk 1 egg with the sugar for about 1 minute, then add the other eggs one at a time, whisking until light and fluffy, about 8 minutes.
4. Add the lemon juice, yoghurt, milk and oil. Beat on high speed until slightly emulsified, about 10 minutes.
5. Fold in the flour mixture and combine well but do not overmix.
6. Pour the batter into the tin. Smooth the top and tap the tin gently on the counter to get rid of air bubbles. Bake for 40 minutes. Leave to cool in the tin.
7. To make the glaze, combine the icing sugar and yoghurt until smooth.
8. Remove the cake from the tin and pour the glaze over, allowing it to drip down the sides. Decorate with edible flowers, lemon zest and a sprinkling of thyme, as illustrated on next page.

Coconut and granadilla bundt cake

Prep time: 20 minutes
Baking time: 50 minutes
Makes: 1 cake

Ⓥ Ingredients

2½ cups (625 ml) flour

½ teaspoon (2½ ml) salt

2 teaspoons (10 ml) baking powder

1 cup (250 ml) unsalted butter, at room temperature

1½ cups (375 ml) castor sugar

6 large eggs

1 teaspoon (5 ml) vanilla essence

¾ cup (190 ml) milk

2 tablespoons (30 ml) desiccated coconut

¼ cup (60 ml) granadilla pulp

For the syrup:

½ cup (125 ml) granadilla pulp

¼ cup (60 ml) castor sugar

1. Preheat oven to 180 °C. Grease a bundt tin.
2. In a medium-sized bowl, sift together the flour, salt and baking powder.
3. In a large bowl, cream the butter and sugar together until light and fluffy using a beater, about 8 minutes.
4. Add the eggs one at a time, beating well after each addition.
5. Add the vanilla essence and milk, and mix to combine.
6. Combine the dry and the wet ingredients and mix until the batter is smooth.
7. Add the coconut and granadilla pulp, and mix.
8. Pour the batter into tin and bake for 45-50 minutes, or until a knife inserted comes out clean. Leave to cool in the tin.
9. To make the syrup, combine the granadilla pulp and castor sugar in a small saucepan set over a medium heat. Bring to a boil, stirring, until the sugar dissolves. Simmer for 2 minutes.
10. Remove the cake from the tin and pour the syrup over, allowing it to drip down the sides.

Homemade custard

Prep time: 20 minutes
Cooking time: 20 minutes
Makes: 2 cups (500 ml)

Ⓥ Ingredients

1½ cups (375 ml) milk
1 cup (250 ml) fresh cream
½ cup (125 ml) castor sugar
1½ teaspoons (7½ ml)
   vanilla essence
6 egg yolks

1. In a small saucepan, heat the milk, cream, ¼ cup (60 ml) castor sugar and vanilla essence, stirring occasionally, until the sugar dissolves completely. Simmer over medium heat till bubbles form around the edges – do not boil. Turn off heat and leave to cool for 15 minutes.
2. In the meantime, combine the rest of the sugar with the egg yolks in a large bowl. Beat well to combine.
3. While whisking, slowly and steadily add three-quarters of the warm cream mixture to the eggs. This slowly raises the temperature of the eggs to prevent them scrambling.
4. Pour the egg mixture into the rest of the cream mixture and return to the heat. Cook over low-medium heat, stirring constantly, to thicken, 5-7 minutes.
5. Strain through a sieve. Serve hot or cold.

No-churn ice creams

Mango ice cream

Prep time: 15 minutes plus 5 hours or overnight in the freezer
Makes: about 4 cups (1 litre)

Ⓥ Ingredients

**3 mangoes, peeled and
puréed**
**1 teaspoon (5 ml) mango
essence**
1 tin condensed milk
**1½ cups (375 ml) fresh
cream, chilled**

1. Combine the mango purée, mango essence and condensed milk.
2. In a separate bowl, whip the cream till soft peaks form, about 3 minutes.
3. Fold the condensed-milk mixture into the whipped cream.
4. Pour into a freezer-safe dish and cover tightly with clingwrap. Freeze for at least 5 hours or overnight.

Oreo ice cream

**Prep time: 15 minutes plus 6-8 hours or overnight in the freezer
Makes: about 3 cups (750 ml)**

Ⓥ **Ingredients**

2 cups (500 ml) fresh cream
½ tin condensed milk
**1 teaspoon (5 ml) vanilla
essence**
6-8 Oreo biscuits, crumbled

1. Pour the cream into a large bowl and whisk till stiff peaks form, about 3 minutes.
2. Combine the condensed milk and vanilla essence, then gently fold into the whipped cream.
3. Pour half of the mixture into a freezer-safe dish, then cover with half the crumbled biscuits. Pour in the rest of the mixture and sprinkle the rest of the biscuits over.
4. Cover tightly with clingwrap, sealing completely. Freeze for 6-8 hours or overnight. (Illustrated on previous page.)

Berry cheesecake ice cream

Prep time: 15 minutes plus 6 hours or overnight in the freezer
Makes: about 3 cups (750 ml)

Ⓥ Ingredients

- 1 cup (250 ml) fresh or frozen blueberries
- 2 tablespoons (30 ml) castor sugar
- ¼ cup (60 ml) water
- 2 cups (500 ml) fresh cream
- 1 tin condensed milk
- 1 teaspoon (5 ml) vanilla essence
- 1 tub cream cheese

1. Put the berries, castor sugar and water in a small saucepan and cook, stirring occasionally, till sugar is dissolved and the fruit is soft, about 15 minutes. Set aside to cool.
2. Pour the cream into a large bowl and whip until stiff peaks form, about 3 minutes.
3. In another bowl, combine the condensed milk and vanilla essence, and mix.
4. Whip the cream cheese until soft, about 3 minutes, then combine with the condensed-milk mixture.
5. Gently fold the cream-cheese mixture into the whipped cream with a spatula, lightly incorporating the two.
6. Spoon half the mixture into a freezer-safe container. Add half the berries. Add the other half of the cream mixture, then the rest of the berries.
7. Cover tightly with clingwrap and freeze for at least 6 hours or overnight. (Illustrated on previous page.)

Tip: Swap out the blueberries for any berries in season.

Chef Jasmine

Chef Coco

Chef Jay

Chef Ivy

Lulu and William

Chef Winnie

10

Alkebulan

Authentic recipes from across the
continent, contributed by some
of my favourite African chefs and
cooks. 'Alkebulan' is the ancient
name of our continent.

Makosso ya Ngulu
(Rwandan pig trotters)

Chef Coco of Epicure

Prep time: 20 minutes
Cooking time: about 3 hours
Serves: 4

Ingredients

½ cup (125 ml) cooking oil
8 cleaned pig trotters
1 medium onion, chopped
1 leek, thinly sliced
1 teaspoon (5 ml) tomato paste
4 green peppers, diced
2 teaspoons (10 ml) grated ginger
3 tomatoes, diced
2 cups (500 ml) water
2 beef stock cubes
salt and pepper to taste

1. In a large pot over medium heat, heat the oil and sear the trotters on all sides for 10 minutes. Remove from pot and set aside.
2. In the same pot, fry the onion and leek with the tomato paste for about 5 minutes.
3. Add the green pepper, ginger and tomatoes. Return the trotters to the pot and mix to coat.
4. Add the water and stock cubes. Cover and reduce heat to very low. Cook until trotters are tender, 2-3 hours.
5. Season with salt and pepper. Serve with pap.

Vinkubala with nshima (Zambian mopane worms with pap)

Lulu and William of @woodkitchen

Prep time: 15 minutes
Cooking time: about 1½ hours
Serves: 4-6

Ingredients
1½ cups (375 ml) vinkubala
   (mopane worms)
4 cups (1 litre) water
1 tablespoon (15 ml) salt
¼ cup (60 ml) oil
1 onion, chopped
1 chilli, chopped
1 clove garlic, minced

For the pap:
3 cups (750 ml) water
2 cups (500 ml) mealie meal
¾ cup (190 ml) cassava meal

For the beans:
1 onion, chopped
1 tablespoon (15 ml) oil
1 tin kidney beans, drained
   and rinsed
125 ml (½ cup) water
salt and pepper to taste

1. Put the vinkubala, water and salt in a pot. Bring to the boil and simmer for 20 minutes. Drain and rinse a couple of times to remove any sand.
2. Heat the oil on high and add the vinkubala. Fry for 10 minutes.
3. Lower heat and add the onion, chilli and garlic, and fry until cooked, 3-5 minutes. Add salt to taste if necessary.
4. To make the pap, bring the water to a boil in a medium-sized pot. Add 1½ cups (375 ml) mealie meal and mix well to combine, breaking up any lumps. Cover and cook for 15-20 minutes. Add the rest of the mealie meal and the cassava meal, and combine well. Reduce the heat and simmer, uncovered, for 20 minutes.
5. To prepare the beans, fry the onion in the oil. Add the beans and water. Simmer for 10 minutes. Season, then mash lightly.
6. Serve the vinkubala with nshima and beans.

Okra
(Zimbabwean ladies' fingers)

Chef Ivy of @a_taste_of_zimbabwe_

Prep time: 10 minutes
Cooking time: 25 minutes
Serves: 4

(V) Ingredients

2 tablespoons (30 ml) oil
1 medium onion, chopped
1 small bird's-eye chilli,
   finely chopped
¾ cup (190 ml) water
1 large fresh tomato,
   chopped
½ teaspoon (2½ ml)
   bicarbonate of soda
5 cups chopped okra (ladies'
   fingers)
salt to taste

1. In a medium-sized saucepan, heat the oil and fry the onion till soft, 2-3 minutes. Add the chilli, ¼ cup (60 ml) water and the tomato, and simmer for 15 minutes.
2. Add the bicarbonate of soda. Bubbles should form.
3. Add the okra and mash lightly with a wooden spoon for 2 minutes as it cooks.
4. Add the rest of the water and season with salt. Cook, beating, until the okra has a sticky consistency, 4-5 minutes. Adjust the seasoning.
5. Serve warm, with pap.

Mandazi
(Kenyan doughnuts)

Chef Jasmine of @cookingwithjaz

Prep time: 20 minutes plus 10 minutes for rising
Cooking time: 30 minutes
Makes: 24 doughnuts

Ⓥ Ingredients

2 cups (500 ml) cake flour, plus extra for kneading

2 teaspoons (10 ml) baking powder

¼ teaspoon (generous pinch) salt

2 tablespoons (30 ml) butter

4 tablespoons (60 ml) sugar

2 teaspoons (10 ml) vanilla essence

½ cup (125 ml) warm water or milk

oil for greasing and deep-frying

1. Sift the flour, baking powder and salt into a bowl.
2. Using your fingertips, rub the butter into the flour until it resembles breadcrumbs.
3. Add the sugar and vanilla essence, and mix.
4. Slowly add the water or milk, mixing until it all comes together as a soft dough.
5. Flour a surface and knead the dough, using your palms, for about 10 minutes.
6. Grease a bowl and put in the dough. Cover with a damp cloth and allow to rise for 10 minutes.
7. Knock down the dough by punching it lightly, and turn it out onto a floured surface. Divide it into 4 portions. Roll out each portion to a thickness of about 2 cm and cut into 6 triangles.
8. Heat the oil and deep-fry in batches until puffed up and golden-brown. Drain on paper towel.

Bofrot
(Ghanaian doughnuts)

Chef Jay of @mukasechic

**Prep time: 10 minutes plus 30 minutes for rising
Cooking time: 30 minutes
Makes: 14 doughnuts**

(V) Ingredients

**3 cups (750 ml) cake flour
½ cup (125 ml) sugar
1 packet instant dry yeast
½ teaspoon (2½ ml) salt
1 teaspoon (5 ml) cinnamon
1 cup (250 ml) lukewarm
    water
oil for deep-frying**

1. Put the flour, sugar, yeast, salt and cinnamon in a bowl. Combine well.
2. Add the water gradually, mixing to make a dough that's stretchy and not too light or too dense.
3. Cover and leave to rise in a warm area until double in size, about 30 minutes.
4. Knock down the dough by punching it lightly, and shape it into 14 equal-sized balls.
5. Heat the oil. Deep-fry in batches until golden-brown and drain on paper towel.

Nigerian baked Jollof rice with shrimps

Chef Winnie of @zeeliciousfoods

Prep time: 10 minutes
Cooking time: 45 minutes
Serves: 6

Ingredients

4 tablespoons (60 ml) tomato paste

3 fresh tomatoes, grated

3 red chilli peppers (tatashe)

2 scotch bonnet peppers (atarodo)

2 large onions, chopped

3 cloves garlic, peeled and minced

2½ cm length root ginger, peeled and grated

1 chicken stock cube, crumbled

½ teaspoon (2½ ml) curry powder

½ teaspoon (2½ ml) thyme

2 teaspoons (10 ml) paprika

¼ cup (60 ml) oil

salt to taste

1 cup (250 ml) long-grain white rice, washed

1 cup (250 ml) frozen mini shrimp

2 cups (500 ml) chicken stock or water

1. Preheat oven to 180 °C.
2. Combine the tomato paste, tomatoes, red chilli peppers, scotch bonnet peppers, onion, garlic, ginger, stock cube, curry powder, thyme, paprika, 2 tablespoons (30 ml) oil and salt. Blend till completely puréed.
3. In an oven-safe pot, heat the rest of the oil. Transfer the purée into the pot and fry for 8-10 minutes or until moisture content dries out. (If you don't have an oven-safe pot, you can use a regular pot, then transfer the fried purée to an oven-safe dish or baking pan.)
4. Add the rice, shrimp and chicken stock or water. Mix to combine.
5. Cover with aluminium foil and bake for 30-35 minutes.
6. Fluff with a fork before serving with fried plantain.

Teff injera (Ethiopian fermented flatbread)

Chef Coco of Epicure

**Prep time: 10 minutes plus 4-5 days for fermenting
Cooking time: 15 minutes
Makes: 8 flatbreads**

Ingredients

**2 cups (500 ml) teff flour
about 5 cups (1¼ litres) water
¼ teaspoon (generous pinch) active dry yeast
oil for greasing**

1. In a large mixing bowl, combine flour, 3 cups (750 ml) water and yeast. Mix well.
2. Cover with clingwrap and make a few holes with a knife. Leave at room temperature for 4-5 days. Add ½ cup (125 ml) water if mixture gets dry.
3. Once it is fizzy and very dark, pour off layer of yeast that has formed on surface, and as much liquid as possible. A clay-like batter remains. Give it a good stir.
4. In a small saucepan, bring 1 cup (250 ml) water to a boil. Stir in ½ cup (125 ml) batter, whisking constantly, until it thickens, about 15 minutes.
5. Stir thickened batter back into fermented batter. Add ⅔ cup (160 ml) water to thin out to consistency of crepe batter.
6. Heat non-stick pan and add a little oil. Spread bottom of pan with batter. Allow it to bubble and let bubbles pop.
7. Cover pan with lid, turn off heat, and steam for 1-2 minutes – do not overcook.
8. Remove with a spatula. Repeat with rest of the batter.
9. Serve with your choice of fillings.

11
Special occasions

Recipes for all celebrations.

Birthday cake

Prep time: 45 minutes
Makes: 1 iced cake

(V) Ingredients

3 Easy vanilla sponge cakes
  (see page 141)
sprinkles to decorate

For the vanilla
buttercream icing:

2 cups (500 ml) unsalted
  butter, at room temperature
4 cups (1 litre) icing sugar
2 teaspoons (10 ml) vanilla
  essence
3 tablespoons (45 ml)
  cream, at room temperature

1. To make the icing, whisk the butter until creamy, about 10 minutes.
2. Add the icing sugar 1 cup (250 ml) at a time, whisking between additions.
3. Add the vanilla essence and cream, and whisk to a smooth and silky consistency, about 10 minutes.
4. Scoop the icing into a piping bag. Ice one cake, then top with the other. Ice the second cake and top with the third. Continue icing till fully covered and decorate with sprinkles.

Rainbow cupcakes

Prep time: 45 minutes
Baking time: 20 minutes
Makes: 12 cupcakes

(V) Ingredients

- 1¼ cups (315 ml) cake flour
- 1¼ teaspoons (6 ml) baking powder
- ½ teaspoon (5 ml) salt
- ½ cup (125 ml) butter, at room temperature
- ¾ cup (190 ml) sugar
- 2 large eggs, at room temperature
- ½ cup (125 ml) amasi or buttermilk or plain yoghurt
- 1 teaspoon (5 ml) vanilla essence

1. Preheat oven to 180 °C. Line a cupcake pan with paper cases.
2. Combine the flour, baking powder and salt in a bowl.
3. In a separate large bowl, using an electric mixer, beat the butter and sugar until light and fluffy, about 5 minutes.
4. Add the eggs one at a time, beating after each addition.
5. Add half the dry ingredients to the wet ingredients, and mix on low speed. Slowly add the amasi and vanilla essence until completely mixed. Add the remaining dry ingredients. Keep whisking until completely mixed, scraping sides of bowl.
6. Scoop the batter into the baking cups, filling each about two-thirds full.
7. Bake for 15-20 minutes or until a toothpick inserted in the centre comes out clean. Leave to cool completely before decorating.

Recipe continued on next page.

For the buttercream icing:

1½ cups (375 ml) butter
4½ cups (1 litre, 125 ml) icing sugar
1½ teaspoons (8 ml) vanilla essence
¼ cup (60 ml) cream
red, blue and yellow food colouring

8. To make the buttercream icing, beat the butter until creamy, about 10 minutes. Add the icing sugar, vanilla essence and cream, and beat until smooth.
9. Divide the icing between 3 bowls, and add a drop of each of the food colourings to each. (To make more colours, combine red and yellow to make orange, blue and yellow to make green, and blue and red to make purple.)
10. Transfer each coloured icing into a small plastic bag and cut off the corner. Lay a single sheet of clingwrap on the kitchen counter, and pipe a line of each icing colour, one at a time and next to each other, to create stripes.
11. Carefully roll up the clingwrap to create a large log of icing, then twist the ends to seal.
12. Prepare a large piping bag with a big star nozzle. Cut off one end of the icing log and insert it, open side down, into the piping bag. Holding the bag vertically, pipe the icing in a spiral onto each cupcake, starting around the outside edge of the cupcake, winding inwards and building height to create a peak (as illustrated on previous page).

Heart-shaped shortbread biscuits

Prep time: 30 minutes plus 20 minutes in the fridge
Baking time: 12 minutes
Makes: 20 biscuits

Ⓥ Ingredients

- **1½ cups (375 ml) butter**
- **1 cup (250 ml) icing sugar**
- **1 teaspoon (5 ml) vanilla essence**
- **2¾ cups (690 ml) cake flour, plus extra for rolling**
- **¼ teaspoon (generous pinch) salt**
- **100 g milk chocolate**

1. Preheat oven to 180 °C. Grease a baking tray.
2. In a large bowl, cream the butter and icing sugar until pale, about 8 minutes.
3. Add the vanilla essence and mix.
4. Sift in the flour and salt, and combine to form a dough. Refrigerate for 20 minutes to make it easier to handle.
5. Flour a surface and roll out the dough to a thickness of 2 cm. Using a heart-shaped cutter, cut out shapes and transfer to baking tray.
6. Bake until golden, about 12 minutes. Carefully transfer to wire rack to cool completely.
7. Melt the chocolate in a bowl over hot water. Dip each biscuit in chocolate and lay on wax paper to set.

Chocolate-dipped strawberries

Prep time: 20 minutes plus 30 minutes for setting
Cooking time: 5 minutes
Makes: 12-16 choc-dipped strawberries

(V) **Ingredients**

150 g chocolate, milk or dark, according to taste, chopped

150 g white chocolate, chopped

1 punnet (12-16) strawberries, stem on

1. Line a baking tray with wax paper.
2. Place the dark chocolate and white chocolate in two different bowls. Melt by putting each bowl over a separate pan of hot water, or in the microwave for 30 seconds at a time, stirring in between.
3. Dip 6-8 strawberries in the dark chocolate by holding the stem, dipping, then twisting and allowing any excess chocolate to drip off. Set on baking tray.
4. Dip a fork into the white chocolate and drizzle over the dipped strawberries.
5. Reverse the process with the other half of the strawberries: dip them into the white chocolate, then drizzle them with the dark chocolate.
6. Set on baking tray. Leave to harden for 30 minutes. (Illustrated on previous page.)

Red velvet cupcakes

Prep time: 25 minutes
Baking time: 20 minutes
Makes: 12 muffin-sized cupcakes

Ingredients

- ½ cup (125 ml) butter
- 1 cup (250 ml) castor sugar
- 2 eggs
- 1 cup (250 ml) buttermilk
- 1 teaspoon (5 ml) vanilla essence
- 2 tablespoons (30 ml) red food colouring
- 2¼ cups (560 ml) cake flour
- 3 tablespoons (45 ml) cocoa
- ½ teaspoon (2½ ml) baking powder
- ¼ teaspoon (generous pinch) salt
- 1 teaspoon (5 ml) bicarbonate of soda
- 1 tablespoon (15 ml) vinegar
- halved strawberries to decorate

For the cream-cheese icing:

- 1 cup (250 ml) icing sugar
- 1 tub cream cheese, at room temperature

1. Preheat oven to 180 ˚C. Grease and line a 12-muffin pan.
2. In a large bowl, cream the butter and castor sugar until fluffy, about 8 minutes.
3. Add the eggs and beat until smooth.
4. Add the buttermilk, vanilla essence and food colouring, and mix.
5. Sift the flour, cocoa, baking powder and salt into a separate bowl.
6. In a third bowl, dissolve the bicarbonate of soda in the vinegar. Stir into the wet ingredients. Don't worry if the batter looks curdled.
7. Fold the dry ingredients into the wet ingredients. Combine well but don't overmix.
8. Spoon the batter into the muffin pan. Bake for 20 minutes. Leave to cool completely before icing.
9. To make the icing, combine the icing sugar and cream cheese. Mix well. Ice each cupcake.
10. Decorate with strawberries, as illustrated on previous page.

Pickled fish

**Prep time: 15 minutes
Cooking time: about 1 hour
Serves: 6**

Ingredients

¼ cup (60 ml) cake flour
salt and pepper to taste
400 g hake, cut into
    medallions
2 tablespoons (30 ml) olive oil
2 large onions, sliced
1 teaspoon (5 ml) grated ginger
1 teaspoon (5 ml) minced
    garlic
2 teaspoons (10 ml) curry
    powder
1 teaspoon (5 ml) turmeric
1 teaspoon (5 ml) cumin
1 teaspoon (5 ml) white pepper
1 tablespoon (15 ml)
    peppercorns
1 tablespoon (15 ml)
    cardamom
3-4 red chillies, deseeded
3 bay leaves
2 tablespoons (30 ml) sugar
3 tablespoons (45 ml) vinegar
¼ cup (60 ml) lemon juice
zest of 1 lemon
½ cup (125 ml) water
3 sprigs thyme

1. In a large bowl, combine the flour, salt and pepper. Coat both sides of each piece of fish, and shake off any excess.
2. Heat 1 tablespoon (15 ml) oil and fry the fish for 2-5 minutes on each side, depending on thickness – do not overcook.
3. Wipe the pan clean, then heat the rest of the oil and fry the onion, ginger, garlic, curry powder, turmeric, cumin and white pepper, about 5 minutes. Remove from the pan and set aside.
4. Place the peppercorns, cardamom, chillies, bay leaves, sugar and vinegar in same pan, and simmer over medium heat until the sugar has dissolved, about 10 minutes.
5. Add the lemon juice, lemon zest, water and thyme, and simmer for another 10 minutes.
6. Return the fish and onion mixture to pan. Toss to coat. Cook for 5 minutes.
7. Transfer to a dish. Leave to cool.

Easter biscuits

Prep time: 15-20 minutes
Makes: 16 biscuits

(V) Ingredients

**1 batch Shortbread biscuits
(see page 140), cut into
Easter-themed shapes
(eg, bunnies, carrots, eggs,
crosses)**
red or pink food colouring
blue food colouring
yellow food colouring

For the royal icing:
2 egg whites
1 cup (250 ml) icing sugar

For egg-free icing:
2 cups (500 ml) icing sugar
**4 tablespoons (60 ml) lemon
juice**

1. To make the royal icing, whisk the egg whites till frothy, about 5 minutes. Add the icing sugar. Whisk till smooth and shiny, about 5 minutes.
2. To make the egg-free icing, combine the icing sugar and lemon juice. Stir well.
3. Divide the icing into four batches, each in its own bowl. Add colours to three of the batches (remember that a little goes a long way – a few drops is all you need). For more colours, combine red and blue for purple, red and yellow for orange, and blue and yellow for green.
4. Scoop the white icing into a piping bag.
5. Ice the cooled biscuits with the coloured icing. Leave to set, then pipe decorations on top with the white icing.

Hot cross buns

**Prep time: 30 minutes plus 35 minutes for rising
Baking time: 20 minutes
Makes: 16 buns**

Ⓥ Ingredients

4 cups (1 litre) cake flour
1 teaspoon (5 ml) salt
½ teaspoon (2½ ml) mixed spice
½ teaspoon (2½ ml) ground cinnamon
4 tablespoons (60 ml) sugar
4 tablespoons (60 ml) butter
1 packet instant dry yeast
1 large egg, beaten
1½ cups (375 ml) lukewarm milk
½ cup (125 ml) sultanas or raisins
2 tablespoons (30 ml) apricot jam

For the paste:
½ cup (125 ml) cake flour
⅓ cup (80 ml) water
2 teaspoons (10 ml) castor sugar

1. Preheat oven to 200 °C. Grease a baking tray.
2. Sift together the flour, salt and spices. Add the sugar.
3. Using your fingertips, rub the butter into the flour mixture.
4. Mix in the yeast.
5. Combine the egg and milk. Mix into the dry ingredients to form a dough.
6. Add the sultanas or raisins.
7. Knead until smooth and elastic, about 8 minutes. Cover and leave to rise in a warm spot till double in size, about 20 minutes.
8. Knock down the dough by punching it lightly, then divide it into 16 pieces and shape each into a bun. Pack the buns closely together on baking tray.
9. Cover and set aside in a warm spot till double in size, about 15 minutes.
10. Make the paste by combining the ingredients, and mixing until smooth. Scoop it into a piping bag, and pipe a cross onto each bun.
11. Bake for 20 minutes.
12. Heat the jam. Remove the buns from the oven and brush them with the jam while still hot.

Malva pudding

Prep time: 10 minutes
Baking time: 40 minutes
Serves: 6

(V) Ingredients

1½ cups (375 ml) cake flour
2 teaspoons (10 ml) baking
powder
½ cup (125 ml) brown sugar
¼ teaspoon (generous
pinch) salt
2 large eggs
1 teaspoon (5 ml)
bicarbonate of soda
1 teaspoon (5 ml) vinegar
3 tablespoons (45 ml)
apricot jam
2 tablespoons (30 ml)
melted butter
¾ cup (190 ml) milk

For the sauce:

1¼ cups (315 ml) cream
⅓ cup (80 ml) butter
⅓ cup (80 ml) sugar
½ cup (125 ml) water
1 teaspoon (5 ml) vanilla
essence

1. Preheat oven to 180 °C. Grease a baking dish or 6 ramekins.
2. Combine the flour, baking powder, sugar and salt in a medium-sized mixing bowl.
3. In a separate bowl, combine the eggs, bicarbonate of soda, vinegar, jam, butter and milk. Mix well.
4. Mix the egg mixture into the dry ingredients until well combined.
5. Transfer batter into baking dish or ramekins. Bake for 30-35 minutes.
6. To make the sauce, combine all the ingredients in a small saucepan. Heat over medium heat, stirring, until sugar has dissolved, about 3 minutes.
7. Remove pudding/s from oven. Pour sauce over while hot and leave to absorb.

Lamb roast

Prep time: 20 minutes plus 1 hour resting
Cooking time: 1 hour, 40 minutes plus 20 minutes resting
Serves: 6

Ingredients

- **3 tablespoons (45 ml) Dijon mustard**
- **2 tablespoons (30 ml) honey**
- **2 teaspoons (10 ml) dried mixed Mediterranean herbs (rosemary, thyme, oregano)**
- **2½ kg leg of lamb**
- **salt and freshly ground pepper to taste**
- **6 potatoes**
- **4 red onions, peeled and quartered**
- **1 garlic bulb, halved**
- **3 tablespoons (45 ml) olive oil**
- **couple of sprigs fresh thyme or rosemary**
- **1½ cups (375 ml) lamb or beef stock**

1. Mix the mustard, honey and herbs together in a bowl.
2. Pat the lamb dry with kitchen paper, and rub with the honey-mustard mixture. Season liberally with salt and pepper. Leave to sit at room temperature, covered, for 1 hour.
3. Preheat oven to 200 °C.
4. Peel the potatoes and slice hasselback style (thinly sliced but left joined at the bottom).
5. Put the potatoes, onion and garlic in a deep roasting pan. Drizzle with olive oil and season with salt and pepper. Add thyme or rosemary sprigs.
6. Place the lamb on a rack over the vegetables. Cook for 20 minutes.
7. Reduce temperature to 180 °C. Pour the stock into roasting pan down the side of (not over) the lamb. Cook for 1 hour and 20 minutes.
8. Remove from oven and transfer the lamb onto a platter. Cover loosely with foil and leave to rest for 20 minutes.
9. Arrange the vegetables on a serving tray. Carve the meat and serve on top of the vegetables.

Honey-glazed gammon

Prep time: 15 minutes
Cooking time: about 1½ hours plus 10 minutes resting
Serves: 6

Ingredients

1 kg gammon
2 bay leaves
1 onion, chopped
2 teaspoons (10 ml) minced garlic
pepper to taste

For the glaze:

2 tablespoons (30 ml) wholegrain mustard
¼ cup (60 ml) honey
¼ cup (60 ml) orange juice
zest of 1 orange

1. Place the gammon in a large pot. Fill with water to cover. Add the bay leaves, onion, garlic and pepper.
2. Bring to a boil, then reduce heat and simmer for 1 hour.
3. Leave to cool in the liquid, then discard the liquid. Remove rind from gammon, and score the fat in diamond shapes with a sharp knife.
4. Preheat oven to 180 ˚C.
5. To make the glaze, put the mustard, honey and orange juice and zest in a small saucepan. Bring to a simmer over medium heat and cook for 5 minutes.
6. Put the gammon in an oven-proof dish. Brush the glaze generously over the gammon, reserving any leftover glaze.
7. Bake the gammon for 20 minutes, brushing with leftover glaze after 10 minutes.
8. Grill the gammon till glossy and golden, 7-10 minutes.
9. Allow to rest for 10 minutes before carving.

Chocolate wreath cake

Prep time: 20 minutes
Baking time: 35 minutes
Makes: 1 cake

 Ingredients

1¾ cups (440 ml) cake flour
2 tablespoons (30 ml) cocoa
  powder
1 teaspoon (5 ml) baking
  powder
½ teaspoon (2½ ml)
  bicarbonate of soda
¼ teaspoon (generous
  pinch) salt
½ cup (125 ml) unsalted
  butter
1 cup (250 ml) sugar
4 eggs
200 g milk chocolate, melted
  in a pan over hot water
2 teaspoons (10 ml) vanilla
  essence
1 cup (250 ml) milk
raspberries and rosemary
  sprigs to garnish

For the chocolate
sauce:
½ cup (125 ml) fresh cream
200 g dark chocolate,
  chopped

1. Preheat oven to 180 ˚C. Generously grease a bundt tin.
2. Sift together the flour, cocoa, baking powder, bicarbonate of soda and salt.
3. In a separate bowl, using an electric mixer, beat the butter and sugar until thick and pale, about 5 minutes. Add the eggs one at a time, beating well after each addition.
4. Gently fold in the melted chocolate until combined.
5. Beating gently, slowly add the flour mixture until combined.
6. Add the vanilla essence and milk, and mix thoroughly.
7. Spoon the batter into the bundt tin, levelling with the back of a spoon. Bake for 30-35 minutes or until a skewer inserted comes out clean. Remove from oven, turn out onto wire rack, and leave to cool completely.
8. To make the chocolate sauce, heat the cream in microwave for 1 minute till hot, then add the chocolate and stir to melt and combine.
9. Drizzle chocolate sauce over cake. Decorate with rosemary sprigs and berries.

Ombre mini mousse trifles

**Prep time: 30 minutes plus 1 hour in the fridge
Cooking time: 4-5 minutes
Serves: 4**

Ingredients

**1 packet Romany Creams
1½ cups (375 ml) cream,
    plus a little extra
1 cup (250 ml) chocolate
    chips
1 tin Caramel Treat
grated chocolate to garnish**

1. Crush the biscuits and divide between 4 dessert glasses. Place in the fridge.
2. Warm ½ cup (125 ml) cream in the microwave and add the chocolate chips. Stir to melt. Whisk until smooth and chocolate has melted completely, about 2 minutes. Leave to cool.
3. In a separate bowl, whisk 1 cup (250 ml) cream until soft peaks form, about 5 minutes. Transfer half of this cream to another bowl and keep in the fridge. Continue whipping remaining whipped cream till stiff peaks form, about 3 minutes.
4. Fold stiffly whipped cream into cooled chocolate mixture in three batches, working gently and quickly.
5. Divide the chocolate mixture between the 4 glasses, layering it on top of the crushed biscuit. Return to the fridge.
6. In a separate bowl, whisk the caramel to loosen it. Add a little cream and beat till smooth, about 2 minutes.
7. Add a layer of caramel on top of the chocolate layer in each of the 4 glasses.
8. Refrigerate for at least 1 hour. Top with reserved whipped cream and grated chocolate.

Summer berry trifle

Prep time: 25 minutes plus 6 hours or overnight in the fridge
Serves: 8

(V) Ingredients

- ¾ cup (190 ml) strawberry or raspberry jam
- 2 cups (500 ml) sliced strawberries
- 2 cups (500 ml) raspberries
- 2 cups (500 ml) blueberries
- 1½ cups (375 ml) whipping cream, cold
- 1 tub cream cheese, at room temperature
- ¾ cup (190 ml) castor sugar
- 1 teaspoon (5 ml) vanilla essence
- 1 packet Boudoir biscuits
- extra berries and fresh mint to garnish

1. Heat the jam in a large bowl in the microwave until hot, about 1 minute. Add the fresh berries and toss to coat.
2. In a separate large bowl, whip the cream until stiff peaks form, about 4 minutes. Set aside.
3. In a separate large bowl, beat the cream cheese with the sugar until smooth, about 3 minutes. Add the vanilla essence and combine well.
4. Add the whipped cream to the cream-cheese mixture in three batches, folding in gently each time, until well combined.
5. Cover bottom of a trifle dish or deep glass bowl with a layer of biscuits, breaking into pieces as necessary. Follow with a third of the berry-jam mixture, then a third of the cream-cheese mixture. Continue layering in this way (biscuits, berry-jam mixture, cream-cheese mixture), ending with the cream-cheese mixture.
6. Garnish with berries and mint. Refrigerate for at least 6 hours.

Christmas cookies

**Prep time: 15 minutes plus 20 minutes in the fridge
Baking time: 12 minutes
Makes: 22-25 cookies**

Ⓥ Ingredients

1½ cups (375 ml) butter
1 cup (250 ml) icing sugar
**1 teaspoon (5 ml) vanilla
essence**
**2¾ cups (690 ml) cake flour,
plus extra for rolling**
**¼ teaspoon (generous
pinch) salt**
sprinkles to decorate

For the icing:
½ cup (125 ml) lemon juice
2 cups (500 ml) icing sugar

1. Preheat oven to 180 °C. Grease a baking tray.
2. In a large bowl, cream the butter and icing sugar until fluffy and pale, about 8 minutes.
3. Add the vanilla essence and combine.
4. Sift in the flour and salt, and combine to form a soft dough. Refrigerate for 20 minutes to make it easier to handle.
5. Flour a surface and roll the dough out to a thickness of 2 cm. Using Christmas-themed cookie cutters, cut out shapes and place on baking tray.
6. Bake until golden, about 12 minutes. Remove from oven and transfer to wire rack to cool completely.
7. Make the icing by combining the ingredients and mixing well until smooth – the icing should be white and thick. Scoop into a piping bag and decorate the cookies.

Acknowledgements

I would like to thank God, my parents, my sister and my niece, and my friends and family, who've been an incredible source of encouragement and support. Your love has carried me safely to this moment. I can't thank you enough for all that you've poured into me.

To my amazing management team at Polar x, thank you for fighting every fight for me, and for creating fertile ground for me to grow and thrive. I appreciate you so much.

To everyone at Jonathan Ball who helped make this book a reality – thank you for the sleepless nights, the dedication and relentlessness that saw us pull this off, from manuscript to this final masterpiece. I'm so grateful for the amazing support and to be collaborating with such a world-class team.

To Wilna, for designing the perfect book. You get me, always! Your work is incredible. Thank you.

To the team who helped bring the food pages to life, Keletso, Donna, Ivan and Thabitha, every day on set with you was a dream – long, long days but all worth it: every single recipe, every shot, just perfect! I couldn't have assembled a better team. Thank you for bringing my vision to life, and for your patience with my obsession with perfection, and your absolute grace and professionalism. Such excellence I'm honoured to have experienced!

To Kallego, who captures me at my best always – thank you for such a beautiful cover and portraits. And thank you to Luhleli for always making me look my best.

To the Woolworths family, who've been such great support and teachers. I continue to learn so much from your attention to detail and your pursuit of excellence in everything you do. It's been the greatest career highlight to work with you.

To Le Creuset, for supplying the most beautiful product to shoot with – thank you for always being there to support me and my work.

To Lamb and Mutton SA, who continue to support me – it's always such a pleasure to work with you.

To Brand South Africa, for the important work you do as custodians of our country's brand and for the support you provide, and to all brands and media for everything you do to amplify the work we do – thank you.

Most of all, to my community, particularly my social-media family who follow @thelazymakoti and are the biggest and greatest cheerleaders – you've enriched my life in ways I can't begin to express. I'm thankful to each and every one of you. Thank you for the constant love and support. This book was put together with you in mind. Enjoy this gift from me to you.

All my love
Mogau

Index

Page numbers in **bold** refer to photos.

© Recipes Mogau Seshoene 2021
© Photographs Mogau Seshoene 2021
© Published edition Jonathan Ball Publishers 2021

Originally published in South Africa in 2021 by
JONATHAN BALL PUBLISHERS
A division of Media24 (Pty) Ltd
PO Box 33977
Jeppestown
2043

ISBN 978-1-92836-315-6
Website: www.jonathanball.co.za
Twitter: www.twitter.com/JonathanBallPub
Facebook: www.facebook.com/JonathanBallPublishers

While every effort has been made to check that the information in this recipe book is correct at the time of going to press, the publisher, author and their agents will not be held liable for any damages incurred through inaccuracies.

Cover, design and typesetting by Wilna Combrinck
Photography by Donna Lewis
Cover and portraits by Katlego Mokubyane
Editing by Tracey Hawthorne
Styling by Keletso Motau
Assistant chefs: Ivan Masiyazi and Thabitha Magwagwa
Proofreading by Gudrun Kaiser
Indexing by Sanet le Roux
Printed and bound by CTP Printers, Cape Town